Praise for UNFRIENDING MY EX

"Reading Kim Stolz's riveting, haunting *Unfriending My Ex*, I found myself wondering, why did it take until 2014—this many years into the technological revolution—for someone to write a book like this?"

—Michael Cunningham, Pulitzer Prize–winning author of *The Hours* and *The Snow Queen*

"In this reader-friendly and cogently argued book, Kim Stolz shares another story—of her digital addiction and how it enslaved her, fraying friendships, and attention spans, and making her and members of her generation less, not more, connected. *Unfriending My Ex* is a punch in the nose, meant not to knock out technology, but to jolt us to seek more balance in our lives. Because it is so personally honest, it will rivet your attention."

—Ken Auletta, author of *Googled*

"Kim Stolz has written an exciting book about love and life in the era of the iPhone. Whether you're addicted to technology or totally anti social media, she captures the reality of living a sexy, busy, buzzy life today. She's the ultimate cool chick, an authentic artist, and a natural-born writer."

—Alyssa Shelasky, author of *Apron Anxiety*

"Stolz explores a topic so current and impactful that I only checked my Twitter and Instagram twice while reading it!"

—Caprice Crane, international best-selling author of *Stupid and Contagious* and *Confessions of a Hater*

"I remain hopeful that despite current trends, self-awareness and genuine human connection are achievable among the 'me' generation. Kim Stolz's *Unfriending My Ex* serves as an entertaining and much-needed reminder that we can live without our phones (temporarily) and that being able to laugh at yourself and learn from your mistakes is crucial if you plan to thrive in this digitally connected, fast-paced society."

—Nev Schulman, host of MTV's *Catfish* and author of *In Real Life*

"As a self-confessed Web-aholic I am well aware that social networks have preyed upon humanity's innate need to connect, and the result is nothing short of a planetary epidemic of info addiction. We are not only content to live in the Matrix but are increasingly driven to be a cognitive cog in its functionality. Kim Stolz has the mind of a scientist in the body of a millennial. Her experiences on reality television and MTV have made her something of a Jane Goodall of digital culture: she lives among them, ever observant, to catalog and understand their behavior patterns while attempting to determine the landscape of Mankind's future."

—**Chris Hardwick, host of Comedy Central's @*midnight* and author of *The Nerdist Way***

"In *Unfriending My Ex*, Kim Stolz gives us a clear-eyed, exceptionally intelligent look at a phenomenon at once mystifying and unavoidable. The thrall in which social media holds us feels so enchanting, we may be losing control of the most valuable parts of our lives to it. The author while respectful of both progress and of her generation, seeks to restore that control. If our times may be defined by a smartphone, we should be grateful that *Unfriending My Ex* is a hell of a lot smarter."

—**Roger Rosenblatt, author of *Rules for Aging: A Wry and Witty Guide to Life***

"It's hard to believe the 1980s once got slapped with the tag the 'Me Decade.' What seemed like a materially indulgent era more than twenty years ago had nothing on the narcissism of the past ten years, the 'iDecade,' if you will, and those who made it so, the 'iGeneration.' That group of look-at-me, listen-to-me, here's-what-I'm-doing-right-now, poke-you, don't-delete-me, I-ought-to-be-famous-just-cuz young people are the subject of Kim Stolz's book. And if anyone ought to know the topic, it's Kim."

—**John Norris, MTV News correspondent**

Unfriending My Ex

———

And Other Things
I'll Never Do

KIM STOLZ

SCRIBNER

New York London Toronto Sydney New Delhi

Scribner
A Division of Simon & Schuster, Inc.
1230 Avenue of the Americas
New York, NY 10020

First Scribner hardcover edition June 2014

SCRIBNER and design are registered trademarks
of The Gale Group, Inc., used under license by
Simon & Schuster, Inc., the publisher of this work.

For information about special discounts for bulk purchases,
please contact Simon & Schuster Special Sales at
1-866-506-1949 or business@simonandschuster.com.

The Simon & Schuster Speakers Bureau can bring authors to
your live event. For more information or to book an event contact the
Simon & Schuster Speakers Bureau at 1-866-248-3049 or
visit our website at www.simonspeakers.com.

Jacket design by Tal Goretsky
Hand-lettering by Janet Hanson
Jacket photograph by Matthias Clamer

Manufactured in the United States of America

1   3   5   7   9   10   8   6   4   2

Library of Congress Control Number: 2013045925

ISBN 978-1-4767-6178-7
ISBN 978-1-4767-6179-4 (ebook)

To my iPhone, without which (whom?)
this never would have been possible.

CONTENTS

Author's Note xi

1 The Experiment 1

2 Generation, Interrupted 31

3 Facebook Is Ruining My Life 57

4 We're "Friends" 79

5 103

6 I Didn't Mean to Do That 123

7 Unfriending My Ex 133

8 Does This Filter Make Me Look Famous? 159

9 Baby Steps 181

Acknowledgments 193

Notes 197

AUTHOR'S NOTE

You're probably going to notice that the names of many individuals in this book are the names of *Beverly Hills, 90210* characters. The characters on these pages reflect people I know and experiences that I have had, but naturally, I made the decision to change names and identifying characteristics. Whether you are now named Brenda, Luke, Donna, Brandon, Kelly, or any other name, no doubt all of you exes, acquaintances, and lifelong pals will think you recognize yourselves (or parts of yourselves), and if you're mad at me and want to hold it against me forever, you are well within your rights to do so. I'll understand if you unfriend me.

Unfriending My Ex

1

The Experiment

When I told my colleagues and loved ones about my idea for this book, that I'd be reflecting on social media and technology and how it has changed us for better or for worse, most of them laughed in my face. Obviously not the reaction you dream of when you set out to write your first book. I bet no one laughed when George Orwell set out to write *Animal Farm*. Apparently the concept of young pigs planning a rebellion is more realistic than my reflecting on the impact of our generation's obsession with social media.

I admit (the first step is admitting) I don't have a lot of "distance" from the issue. I may be one of the most digitally obsessed and addicted people of my generation. I also acknowledge that my former career as an on-air host for MTV as well as my notoriety as "the gay one" from *America's Next Top Model* were enabled and heightened by the reality television craze, the blogosphere, and outlets like Facebook, Instagram, Tumblr, Twitter, and even Myspace and Friendster (RIP). I also am aware that I unabashedly used these tools to promote the restaurant I owned, the Dalloway (singles' night, girls' night, "Rosie from *Real Housewives* is coming!," etc.). I have been kept in the public eye thanks to these electronic avenues, and much of my success has been a by-product of technological preoccupations.

So, sure, I get why they laughed (are still laughing). But I'm an intrepid author, and I live to serve, so I decided to undertake an experiment for the public good. It was an experiment to prove to them (and maybe to myself too) why this book had to be written.

The parameters of the experiment were as follows: no iPhone or use of any other smart phone, no Internet (which meant no Facebook, Instagram, Twitter, or any other social media), no AIM, no Gchat or e-mail, and no DVR (I allowed myself television, but no reality shows). I gave my precious iPhone to my roommate, Kelly, who locked it up, so I knew I wouldn't crumble from temptation—especially after a couple glasses of wine.

I prepared for my experiment assiduously, planning as if I were being transported to 1854 to live the rest of my days at Walden Pond with only my deliberations to keep me company. It wasn't going to be the rest of my life; it was only going to be a week. But it was going to be a pure week, a week of healthy detox, and I was ready.

Of course, the day before the experiment, full panic set in. I started to have paranoid fantasies about being abandoned by everyone I knew. To alleviate my panic, I spent a hundred dollars on a landline, which was only fair and realistic, considering every household had one before the Internet took over the world. I scribbled down about forty people's numbers that I might need over the course of the week—my friends, my mom and dad, my own landline number (so that I could tell everyone so they would call me), my boss, the MTV hair and makeup department, and the number for the nearest AT&T store (in case I went into full breakdown mode and had to buy a quick iPhone replacement—I knew this would be cheating, but I was terrified). The idea of having a landline proved strangely thrilling. I felt like Carrie Bradshaw when I checked my messages each evening after coming home. In fact, it turned out that checking messages was so exhilarating that after my experiment, I decided to keep the landline. I still have it today. I have yet to receive a single message on my answering machine that isn't from a telemarketer, but I maintain hope.

I was working at the Times Square offices of MTV at the time and would go in for a few hours a day to shoot my segments, but since the terms of the experiment precluded me from using any computers or going on e-mail, I had to ask a production assistant to print out all of the scripts for me. I'm sure my experiment ruined someone's week.

After work, I'd sit on the couch restlessly flipping through a book or magazine and could swear I kept seeing a bright light on the cushion beside me, the clear and exhilarating pop-up light of an iPhone message notification.

I would reach for it over and over, even though I knew it was locked away. Sometimes I'd be watching television and would silently and mindlessly pat the couch, feeling around for my phone. My iPhone was a phantom limb. Every minute or so, my eyes would dart across the room and my hands would search unconsciously for the precious machine, my lifeline. I missed it so much.

I spent the first couple of days in a fugue state: *I wonder what people are doing. I'll just check my—oh no, I can't. Is everyone hanging out right now? Maybe I'm missing something at work. Do I still have friends? I wonder if they've posted about me. What if it's a terrible photo? What if it's a great photo and I can't #regram it? I wonder if something fun is going on that I don't know about.* Who am I? What a mess.

Five, six, or seven hours a day would go by when I wouldn't hear from *anyone*. My coworkers and friends usually sent me hundreds of e-mails each day, and I was used to texting nonstop with twenty or thirty people at a time. But all of a sudden, there was nothing. Nothing except me and my thoughts and my landline.

Sure, I missed the actual people, but truth be told, the anxiety about disconnecting from the chatter was worse. At first I concluded that my phone had been filling a void, but then I realized that was the whole problem: These devices *never* filled a void because *there had never been a void*. They just came in and pushed other, real stuff out. Before smartphones and social media came into all our lives, nothing had been missing. There were books and thoughts and movies and people and places. Now there was just checking your phone every five (two) minutes. There was the twitching and the compulsion, and it really didn't matter who the human being on the other side of the exchange or post or "like" was, just that they were doing it, feeding the beast of self-regard.

It was a moment of clarity.

And then it was over. And I missed my iPhone again.

And so the week went on. Just like with any recovery from addiction, there is an epiphany and there is backsliding. I'm not proud, but I had my addict lows. At one point in the first couple of days, I couldn't help myself and went into Kelly's room to try to find my phone. I just really wanted to text *someone, anyone*—I just wanted my phone with me again. I thought, *I can cheat one time. Nobody will know*, which was totally ridiculous, because if I texted a friend, they would obviously know! Like a crazy person, I looked through all of Kelly's stuff and tried to find my precious phone, but I couldn't. I couldn't even text her photos of the amazingly embarrassing things I was finding in her room! Later, I admitted all of this to her, and without registering surprise, she told me she had taken it to work with her. "I know you," she said. "There was no way I was leaving that phone in my room for you to find."

My anxiety astounded me. I even got the shakes a few times. My friend Dr. Amy Wicker (a real person, not a *90210* character), who happens to be a clinical psychologist in New York City, explained to me that withdrawal is defined as a "syndrome of painful, physical and psychological symptoms that follow the discontinuance of an addicting

5

substance," and although I didn't feel *pain* per se, I definitely suffered both physical and psychological symptoms. Dr. Wicker added that while a smartphone is not considered an "addictive substance," it is possible that one could experience significant emotional distress associated with an unfulfilled compulsion to check one's phone, most notably a sharp rise in anxiety levels. Even though the psychological community does not yet officially recognize my addiction, I *felt* otherwise.

Fortunately, as the week progressed, the frequency of these mini panic attacks lessened from every few minutes to about every thirty minutes, then every few hours, and eventually not at all. Watching TV helped quell the panic. But then my missing DVR sent me onto a whole other slide of anxiety. I was watching some good old-fashioned, real-time television, and I would press the "fast forward" button incessantly, not able to fully compute why the commercial played at normal speed. You've probably gleaned by now that I like instant gratification; I like to see results and I absolutely hate waiting. I am completely incapable of watching television shows in real time. When I have guests over to my house and we decide to watch a show and the commercial comes on, I watch in awe as these people lower the volume and talk among themselves as if this is a completely acceptable thing to do. It's not okay for me. I don't even care about what happens next in the show (especially because I'll miss half of it due to incoming texts and intervals of Instagram scrolling); I care about not waiting for it.

Reverting to watching TV in real time was torture. Experiencing commercials is boring; it is also expensive. Do you know how hard it is to not buy what is being sold to you when you have nothing else to do but watch it? I bought two stand-alone elliptical machines that had no railings, just the little foot pedals. I bought them because they wouldn't take up much space and the commercial told me I would get in shape. I bought a second one because I thought I would be lonely doing it by myself. When they came in the mail, I set them up and got on. I fell off and twisted my ankle. No railings! Three hundred forty-nine dollars later, they still collect dust in my closet.

Now that I was watching commercials, I noticed how many of them were devoted to telecommunication companies and the products and services they sell. It was like having to watch someone I had just broken up with star in five two-minute shows each hour. I missed my iPhone so much. Television is boring when you can't IMDb that random actor you loved from *Twin Peaks* but whose name you can't remember (Leland!) and text friends about how strange *American Idol* has become or what Walter White is going to do next.

Suddenly I had time on my hands. So what did I do? I decided to try to read a book. I know . . . revolutionary. I set my sights on Henry David Thoreau's *Walden*. I may have been a bit optimistic about getting through a tome that dense in a week, but I had loved it in high school and I wanted to see if it still seemed as relevant and thrilling as an adult. Plus, I felt like I would relate to it; Thoreau spent two years in a cabin and I was spending a week without social media. I was getting as pathetically close to a Walden Pond–type experience as you really can in this day and age.

If you aren't familiar with it, *Walden* is part social experiment, part voyage of spiritual discovery. Thoreau chronicles two years he spent in a cabin he built in the woods. Basically, by removing himself from his social context, he was able to achieve a deeper understanding of himself, the world around him, and on and on. He set out to Walden to live "deliberately," to "simplify, simplify" and thus enrich his life. I was basically Henry David Thoreau living in the twenty-first century. (Mrs. Smith, my dear tenth-grade English teacher, if you are reading this, please forgive me for comparing myself to Thoreau. I know I have no right.)

Confession (sorry again, Mrs. Smith): I hadn't read a full book in a really long time—not including *Twilight*, which I had to read when I covered the *Twilight* trilogy at MTV. Even when I was reading that lighter fare, I was *still* easily distracted by whatever was around me. In fact, one of the most tangible changes in my life due to my addiction and increasingly distracted nature is that my attention span is shot. I am basically incapable of reading a single article in the newspaper or a chapter of a book in a single sitting.

One of my favorite weekend activities used to be lounging around and reading the *New York Times* and *Wall Street Journal* front to back. My dad and I used to sit in the living room, read a paper each, then switch and read the other. Now, we sit down with our reading (usually via the app on our iPads) and within twenty minutes we're playing online Hearts via Bluetooth. These days, when I try to read, I generally get through the first line of each paragraph before my eyes start to skim and my fingers reflexively turn the page. I interrupt my "reading" every few minutes to check my iPhone. I usually make it through one or two articles but give up because I realize I'm not retaining anything. Sometimes I'll manage to get through an entire article but realize I absorbed absolutely nothing because I spent the entire time thinking about the person who wasn't texting me back . . . or how to respond to the person who was. If you're anything like me, your eyes probably glazed over midway through this last paragraph. In fact, you're probably texting right now, aren't you? That's okay. I totally get it.

Needless to say, at first it was difficult for me to focus on *Walden*. I had to read paragraphs over and over, because my mind was stuck in this rut: *I have to check my phone*. But after, once the phantom iPhone limb started to haunt me less frequently, I adjusted, and slowly but surely my attention span and focus came back. Suddenly, I was absorbing everything. And what's more, I was enjoying it. Thoreau's transcendentalist journey brought him self-reliance and self-sufficiency. He did not have to see company or hear a phone beep to feel confident or secure. He wrote:

> I wanted to live deep and suck out all the marrow of life, to live so sturdily and Spartan-like as to put to rout all that was not life, to cut a broad swath and shave close, to drive life into a corner, and reduce it to its lowest terms, and, if it proved to be mean, why then to get the whole and genuine meanness of it, and

publish its meanness to the world; or if it were sublime, to know it by experience, and be able to give a true account of it in my next excursion.

Those lines played over in my mind, even though the phrase "cut a broad swath" has always inexplicably made me cringe. On one level, I'd embarked on the experiment as a way to show my friends and family that I could do without my obsessive connection. But on a deeper level, I wanted to understand life on my terms again, to feel my feelings, whether positive or excruciatingly negative, and I wanted my time back, all the hours that I spent texting or Facebooking or tweeting. I wanted to get this experiment right so that afterward, in the coming weeks, months, and years, for the rest of my life, I would be able to see life in its raw form and so learn to live my life with less interruption and more deliberateness. But once I got into the thick of the experiment and I felt so alone and panicky, I started to get pretty bearish on the whole thing. Thoreau seemed to be better at this than me.

And then something changed . . .

It happened around day four. Suddenly, I found myself a little bit closer to Thoreau. I was walking more slowly everywhere I went. The words *leisurely pace* occurred to me. Things were starting to actually occur to me! I was looking around, noticing people, their faces, emotions, appearances, and style. I felt as if I hadn't been down my own street for years. It reminded me of when I got my first pair of glasses in sixth grade—I walked outside and looked at a big tree and *really* saw the tree. All the details that I had been missing amazed me. I hadn't realized that I couldn't see. Other things started coming into focus too. I was listening in meetings, engaging my friends in genuine conversations that lasted more than thirty seconds, and reading magazines and newspapers, which for the last two years I had complained I didn't have time to read but had actually stopped reading because I could not concentrate on them. In fact, I always had the time but had wasted an estimated *four and a half hours per day* on my phone! Four and a half hours—time I could have spent reading several chapters of a novel, writing a blog, doing work, calling my grandparents, having a much-needed conversation with a friend or significant other, or even going to the gym (okay, probably not the gym). I did the math, and it was even more alarming: At that point, I had owned a smartphone for more than six years, and my addiction to it cost me roughly 9,855 hours. That's *411 days*. Well over a *year*! And it had left me with a less-than-satisfactory ability to read, an obnoxiously low attention span for my friends and family, and an almost complete unawareness and disavowal of the world around me.

I recalled how one night, I was eating dinner with a friend who had recently broken up with the boyfriend she had been with since college. He had cheated on her after years of dating, so her tears were in no short supply. In the middle of analyzing the post-breakup texts the ex had sent to her, I picked up my glass of sauvignon blanc, and, behind it, a pop-up message on my iPhone caught my eye.

Thus began the familiar itch—including the twitching minor anxiety that I was missing something good. I began imagining all of the exciting things that the pop-up message could portend, and before I could snap back to the conversation, my urge to check turned into a complete loss of attention. For a moment I even forgot that I was, in fact, at dinner, listening to a friend in the middle of a crisis. I took a deep breath and reflected on the situation. It was eight P.M. on a Sunday night, so the likelihood that the message was signaling an important work e-mail or anything at all that would demand an immediate response was minuscule. Still, I was fighting a powerful urge to check and felt a cold sweat building up on the back of my neck.

A good friend would have ignored her phone. Make that: a good friend would *not* have had her phone on the table. I had always prided myself on being caring and attentive, but over the previous few years I had received countless complaints from friends and family about the fact that I *never* put my phone down during meals or face-to-face conversations (I can see my friends reading this and nodding their heads in affirmation right now). Knowing full well that I would be reprimanded but still too engrossed to come up with a better excuse, I used the same line I had a thousand times before:

"Ugh I'm sorry, this is probably work. I just have to check to make sure it isn't my boss . . . Just one sec—"

This was the seventh dinner in three weeks during which I had recognized that my catching a glimpse of the light on my phone was quickly followed by the compulsion to check. Of course, when I gave in to the itch I found junk e-mails: Wasabi Lobby's sushi specials, Pottery Barn's seasonal sale, a pop-up notification about the score of a sporting event that I didn't even know was happening, or the five-times-per-day AccuWeather alert, warning me about a coastal flooding watch (is there always a coastal flooding watch? So confused about this) in my area.

It had happened a million times before, but it didn't matter. The off chance that the message could be exciting, dramatic, tragic, or life-changing (or from an ex!) was just too tempting and caused an almost-thirty-times-hourly "need" to check my phone. And so I welcomed my one-week switch from a smartphone to a landline. It was going to make me a better person, I was sure of it.

Having a landline during my experiment didn't only help with my ability to be present at dinners and meetings. I also found that there is a stark difference in talking on a landline compared to talking on a smartphone—that is, if one even talks on a smartphone at all and doesn't just text. I found that the landline encouraged longer conversations. It also felt like a novelty, so in a way these conversations seemed more special. I was brought back to the days when I would lie on my bed and talk to my friends for hours on the phone. (Remember in the opening credits of *Beverly Hills, 90210* when Kelly is lying and rolling on the bed on her landline?! Just like that! Except for the rolling part because no one does that! But you get what I'm saying.) Most importantly, I was less distracted because I didn't have a multitude of messages coming and going across the screen while I tried to concentrate on what the person on the other end was saying. I forgot how exciting and lovely it could be when the phone would ring and it was a *surprise* to find out who was on the other end, how nice it was to hear my phone ring without getting a text beforehand that said *Can I call you?* (Is there a more ridiculous waste of time than that text? Isn't the ring the universal symbol of *Can I call you?*) I had to actually talk to people when they called, and I rediscovered how wonderful this kind of interaction could be. It was great to *hear* people's reactions, rather than just read the *haha* or *lol* or *imagine?!* or *omg what?!* It was as if I had forgotten there was a living, breathing, feeling person behind those digital letters and emoticons. In only one week, these conversations strengthened my friendships with people with whom I usually communicated through text or social media.

My evenings changed that week as well. In general, my nights usually consisted of a dinner and two or three stops afterward, at least two of which I would finalize over text once I was already out (if I was drinking, I would make plans to go to five and end up at one plus the Pisa Pizza around the corner from my apartment). But during my experiment, I made one plan, confirmed in advance over the phone, and once I was at my destination, I could devote all of my attention to being there instead of thinking about where I was heading next.

I know that I missed events and get-togethers because I wasn't on e-mail, text, or Facebook, but I didn't feel left out because whatever I was doing, I was wholly immersed in it. I wasn't distracted enough to care about what my *other* friends were up to that night. I was able to enjoy what I was doing rather than wondering whether the twenty other events or hangouts I knew were happening that night would have been more fun. And the best part was that I couldn't see on social media all of the amazing things my friends were doing and how many of them were hanging out without me. Ignorance was bliss. The information overload was gone.

My romantic relationship fared better too. We weren't relying on incessant texting, e-mailing and Gchatting—where messages lack tone and often lead to confusion and conflict, or worse, lend themselves to unexpected minute- or hour-long lags in conversation that can send you down a rabbit hole of panic—so we had far fewer misunderstandings.

I tend to "talk" a lot faster over text, which often means that much less thought and much more impulse seep into my responses and comments, and they don't always read as humorous, especially if I take only a few seconds to compose them. I'm most clever and witty in the beginning of relationships because I take time and put real thought into my responses, whether they be over e-mail, text, or Gchat. As relationships progress, however, we all begin to care a little bit less about the impression we make because, well, the first has already been had. I take less time with what I say, and in texts that means jotting down the first thought that comes into my head. My comments aren't well crafted anymore. It's just what happens when you're texting one hundred to one hundred twenty times per day.

Believe it or not I have passable social skills in person and on the phone. But in texts, it seems that every single thought that comes into my head ends up on the virtual page (it's much easier to type terrible things than to actually say them!). So now, with our smartphones and e-mail out of the equation, my girlfriend at the time and I did not argue once (okay, we argued *once*, but that's pretty good!). And because we were communicating less frequently during the day, we were more excited to see each other and recount the stories from our respective days. Our nightly reunions seemed like an old television show, as if I were Desi in *I Love Lucy* coming home after work and exclaiming, "Honey, I'm home!" (Also, I recently found out that my mom once went on a date with Desi Arnaz Junior? She's so much cooler than I am. But anyway, I digress.)

One day during my experiment, I was talking on my landline to a friend six years my junior who was studying for her foreign relations midterm at NYU. We were discussing one of President Nixon's policies when she told me she had been absent the day her professor had covered it in class. She didn't seem anxious about this at all, whereas I remembered how I would manically attempt to get every classmate to share their notes with me from any class I'd missed so I could be fully prepared and then would talk to the professor during office hours, just to be safe. Perhaps I was on the extremely meticulous end of the curve, but I was still alarmed to hear my friend's indifference. "I can just read about all of it online," she told me. "I don't need to be in class to find out what Nixon's policies were." She was certainly right, but I was also in the midst of an Internet detox, so I was acutely aware of the hazards of technology. What if she wasn't getting her information from accurate and reliable sources? And what did that say about how we valued professors if we disregarded their crucial role in education? Certainly the man or woman teaching her course was better regarded in his field than Wikipedia. Wikipedia, of course, is notoriously unreliable. I once checked my own Wikipedia page to find out that I had died the week before. It was a very existential experience. And it marked the only time I modified or wrote anything on my Wikipedia profile—it seemed like bad luck to be dead on the Internet.

But while I scoffed at the notion of replacing a professor with a basic Google search, I quite commonly forewent a doctor's visit in favor of trip to WebMD. One day during my experiment, I woke up with a very strange pain in my neck. On any other day I would have typed my symptoms into a search engine to find a name for my ailment (which more often than not would come up as leukemia, cancer, or AIDS). Now, as I was banned from the Internet, I had no choice but to do things the old-fashioned way: pick up the phone and call my physician. (I even had to call 411 first, as his number was stored in my iPhone.) After just a few minutes on the phone, Doc prescribed me some medication, and I felt better in a day or two. I was alarmed that the ease and simplicity (and lack of expense) of conducting a Google search had often replaced the wise counsel and expertise of people who'd actually been trained to diagnose medical ailments. I could have saved myself a lot of anxiety about small pains that could metastasize into brain cancer if I'd bothered to pick up the phone and call an MD rather than typing "neck pain and cancer symptoms" into my browser. The Internet is a great equalizer. But it's useful to remember that just because someone has a domain name doesn't mean he or she is an actual, qualified expert who can tell you whether your life is basically over.

After my doctor cured me of my neck cancer, which was actually just a pinched nerve easily addressed by a few pills and a great massage masking itself as a physical therapy appointment, I settled in to work on an article. I was writing it by hand, on actual lined, loose-leaf paper—I didn't trust myself to use my computer—and needed some information on a particular policy. Normally I might have just taken my question to the Web, but this time I called my friend who happened to be a government professor at Columbia. Having had a real conversation with a (reliable and credentialed) human being, I didn't have to cross-check my facts against three different online sources because of the risk that some whack job had made something up on his website. And even better, I got to catch up with a friend and discuss something that we both found interesting. Imagine.

The entire week I found that I was exercising my mind much more frequently, thinking of answers to questions that ordinarily I would have found on my smartphone. I also relied on my brain to do math—tipping a waiter, basic addition and subtraction—when in any other case I would have pulled out my phone for the same purpose—despite the fact that I'm actually really good at math.

Why should we retain any real information? The preamble to the Constitution? Look it up online! Multiplication tables? There's an app for that! I had gotten so dependent on my iPhone and Gmail calendars to tell me when I had appointments that during the experiment I missed two meetings, four casting calls, two auditions, and one potential freelance assignment. This lapse in memory isn't just because I'm getting older—it's happening to most of us. Apparently, short-term memory loss is one of the many widespread effects that smartphones, social media, and the Internet have had on our minds. According to a *San Francisco Chronicle* article, our dependence on smartphones for even "the simplest programs—such as spell-checker . . . are short-circuiting the brain's ability to process details." Some people have forgotten how to spell simple words because they know the program they are using will catch any errors. In college I was able to rely on my memory for important dates, but I can't do that anymore. (At least I can still spell. I really am a great speller. Thank you, Brearley!)

After only one week unplugged, I realized what an incredibly high percentage of my exchanges with my friends were about reality television shows and reality stars, and was astounded that by missing just one week of television (about two hours per night), I was useless in at least half of the discussions that took place around me. My week of detox happened right around the time that everyone was obsessed with watching YouTube videos about kittens. Remember that? What a terrible time in America. I sat down to dinner with a few coworkers and friends and was inundated with blow-by-blow accounts of the best kitten videos of the day. I'll admit it, I am not a cat person (i.e., I hate cats), but even if I were, having been detached from YouTube, Facebook, and Twitter, where everyone was sharing these videos, this still would have seemed like an outrageous dinner topic. I guess I had liked "Panda Sneeze" (the mom was so surprised!) and the grape crushers video (that painfully tragic but hilarious moan!), but even those YouTube videos I once blasted to everyone I knew seemed uninteresting now that I had begun to live my life as Thoreau had prescribed. Everyone also wanted to talk about Snooki (remember her? Man, she really fell off the map hard). At some point, I found myself unable to remember whether or not Snooki was a kitten or the *Jersey Shore* girl. That was probably a low (high?) point. Before reality television, I would discuss politics, film, and relationships with these same friends; we rarely had in-depth conversations about television. Sure, we talked about celebrities back then, but they didn't dominate our interactions. After a few days off-line, our celeb-obsessed conversations unsettled me on so many levels; I knew my friends were smart and funny, but these discussions made us seem . . . dumb.

Beyond regaining the ability to read a book and rekindling an interest in something other than Miley's Instagram account, I suddenly felt less antsy. To be honest (TBH), I'm someone who has a relatively high level of anxiety. That's my nature. And for me, the constant possibility of receiving news—good or bad—through the device in my pocket makes me feel even more worried, agitated, distracted, and uneasy. Even if I stopped going through my phone every few minutes and set a regular time to check for e-mail or texts, I would probably start getting anxious three hours before.

In any relationship—romantic, platonic, or work-related—I feel an anxious obligation to reply instantaneously to a message that the other person knows I've read. I'm frequently tortured by the "read receipt" function on iPhones. If the people I'm messaging have theirs turned on, I can see that they have read my message and, if so, when. I check my phone constantly to see if the person has sent any sort of reply or is typing me back or is just completely ignoring me. I can't fully capture in words the agony of seeing that someone read your message fifteen to twenty minutes ago and has not yet written you back. But what really leads me down an ugly path is when I've texted someone and gotten no response, and then I see them post a status update about something like being stuck in traffic on Facebook or upload a photo of the pretty clouds in the sky to Instagram. Are you kidding me? What a virtual slap in the face. I get completely irrational. And I tend to confront—regardless of the potential for awkwardness or friction. Then it gets really bad. I text them saying that I know they're near their phone because I've seen the Instagram upload. Once they receive that, undoubtedly they don't respond again . . . ever. Because I've just made myself look like an obsessed, desperate freak. (But I'm not! The Internet did this to me.)

My wife and I don't fight frequently, but when we have an argument over text, it is much, much more frustrating than in person. Not only do read receipts make us stay glued to our phones, waiting to see when the other has read our most recent jarring jab, but we can also play games with it. I think she would admit doing this as well (if she doesn't do this, then I'm really backing myself into a corner here) but once in a while, when I'm feeling especially frustrated, I will turn off read receipts on my phone. That way, I can read the midst-of-battle texts (and then the predictable "Where did you go?" and "Why aren't you responding?") without giving her the gratification of knowing that I have read and been affected by them. Disabling read receipts is just one of many ways you can manipulate someone with your smartphone. It's terrible. It's sick! It's brilliant. It's not the way I want to be treated, and it's not the way I want to treat people. But in the heat of a fight, when you're not quite the most amazing version of yourself, it's easy to slip into these kinds of evil tactics.

Yep, my smartphone usually has a lot of control over me, but the week of my detox, I could take a walk outside and know that nothing could change my emotional state with the press of a button or blink of a light.

After the first painful days, I was able to live a more positive and deliberate life. However, that wasn't true of my glued-to-their-phone-type friends. After alerting people in my life that I would be without my iPhone for the next seven days, one of my friends sent me this e-mail:

> WHY do you think its ok to not warn me about this shit!?! HOW AM I SUPPOSED TO FIND YOU?? Do you have a landline? Do you know Morse code? Can you send smoke signals from your balcony?? I'm in a confined space on the subway and this is not the setting I'd choose for the panic attack I'm currently experiencing. Please let me know.

Interestingly enough, this particular friend who was so desperate to stay in touch didn't call my landline all week. Years later, she and I laughed about how I obsessively called her the entire week without a single call back from her. She lived on text and Facebook, and so despite the fact that she was so freaked out that I was "going away," she still didn't communicate with me in a meaningful way. She didn't miss "me"; she missed "digital me." Once I was off the digital grid, she kind of forgot I existed.

As long as you have a stream of conversations going on online or many people looking at your profiles and liking your posts, it's easy to feel like you are connected and liked and loved. But all of those micro-communications about . . . nothing: What do they really amount to? What do they leave you with at the end of the day? You're not building or deepening relationships. You're just chattering.

The friendships I maintained during my experiment—with people I spoke to on my landline and in person—were solid and real. I really *connected with* the people I was talking to, and that made me feel more grounded in the world, a little more human. A little more like my buddy Thoreau. Yep, just called him my buddy.

Those seven days made me appreciate the little things again. Spending time with my friends, reading books and full articles in newspapers, savoring quiet moments of contemplation, having an awareness of the world around me—I was fully present within my experiences.

Of course—and I was naïve to think it could have been any different—just a few days after my cleanse ended, I went right back to my old ways. I had so many ideas and hopeful dreams about disconnecting on a regular basis and had made all these promises to myself, but the siren song of my iPhone was just too strong. At the end I was left merely with the knowledge of how things could be, how I wanted them to be, even if I was not able or ready to truly change my lifestyle. Thoreau would have been so disappointed.

Being without a cell phone made me think of Confucius's famous saying "No matter where you go, there you are." During my experiment, wherever I was, whatever I was doing, I was *there*. Nothing—no texts, calls, e-mails, or television—could pull my focus. I was fully present. I felt each thought, fear, self-reflection, and insecurity as it occurred.

But the week after, reunited with my phone, I wasn't truly focusing on anything at all. I could escape any uncomfortable situation—or any situation at all—by texting a friend or checking Facebook or Twitter or Instagram or

Tinder or Tumblr. (I freely admit that when I've run out of social media to check I have also been known to Google myself.) After a full week of focusing on the here and now, I was checking my phone every few minutes; I was texting dozens of people at once. It felt terrible. Introspection was dead (again). My interactions with other people consisted mainly of half conversations in which I would smile, nod, and say *Yeah* or *Wow, that's amazing*, having no idea what they'd actually said because I was too engulfed by the stream of texts, e-mails, and instant messages on my phone.

My social media and phone addiction has metastasized as the years have passed. I have owned two Nokias, two PalmPilots ('memba those?), four BlackBerries, three iPhones, and two iPads, all of which I treated like newborn children and none of which I could go without for more than thirty minutes at a time. (Or, more honestly, five or six minutes. Fractions of minutes.) I can't help but laugh when I think back to what I used to consider "addicted" and "dependent" behavior when it came to simpler talk-and-text cell phones—or even my beeper in high school! I loved that beeper! It was see-through! And I could text my girlfriend 143143143 to let her know I was thinking of her, and there was no way for those numbers to lead to an all-out text battle. Those early devices were just my gateway. Then I got my first BlackBerry at the end of 2006 and learned the uses (and misuses) of instant e-mail, BBM, the Internet, and Gchat on a mobile device.

While I was gazing at my phone year after year, the

social media stratosphere was changing and expanding. Friendster (RIP) gave way to Myspace (basically RIP), and Facebook modified its policies to include everyone—not just college students. And then Twitter and Instagram and Tinder and Tumblr were born. (Seriously, I have to stop writing about Tinder—I can already feel a livid text from my wife on its way.) Through social media, we could now hear "firsthand" the thoughts and feelings of celebrities. We knew what kinds of fur pillows Kanye liked and the fact that he loved Persian rugs and cherub imagery (thank God he stopped writing about that). Reality television swallowed scripted programming. You could follow real-life drama minute by minute. We were all connected, twitching with near-constant anticipation of what would happen next, who would say or text what, instigated and propelled by the never-ending stream of information.

My parents' generation has watched these new forms of communication and entertainment infiltrate our society, but for a while they denounced this new media as a negative distraction or wrote it off as something they didn't understand, like heavy metal music or obscure indie films or college kids' obsession with David Lynch. At first our parents looked at our social media and smartphone use with the same expression they bore that awkward moment when you came home from college with a boyfriend or girlfriend with sleeves of the tattoo variety. Even now, as older generations have also begun to become obsessed with and addicted to social media and smartphones, it's still significant that they have spent the vast majority of their lives *off-line*, where the greatest degree of their persona-building and important decision-making took place. Their friend-ships and (at least first) marriages did not begin, thrive, or end because of Facebook—though more recently, many in their generation are getting divorced and mentioning Face-book as a culprit. But still, the nuances of their lives weren't chronicled on a twenty-four-hour news feed from the time they were born until they were in an assisted living home where Matty B decided to film his viral YouTube music video. (My grandmother is actually in a Matty B video.) There was a *purity* to their lives then.

When my mother started using Facebook, she often forgot her password and didn't sign in for days at a time. My father is obsessed with his iPad and its magazine and newspaper applications (and of course with Hearts Online) but doesn't frequent many of the communication apps (ex-cept for SnapChat. He loves SnapChat). There was also that three-month stint in 2010 when he became compulsively obsessed with Foursquare and full disclosure: He did up-load his first Instagram a few months ago. It was of a Ger-man couple he'd never met getting married on a float. It remained his only post for months. It was very strange.

But something eventually broke and now he posts pic-tures of our family dog and his steak dinners just like ev-eryone else. From the day I sat down to write this book to the present day, both my parents have let the social media addiction take over. But the difference is that they *can* put it down when they need to and their lives haven't been molded and shaped and severely affected by it. They enjoy it. It's a pastime, no more, no less.

So that's how my parents react to social media. And conversely there's our generation. A girlfriend once broke up with me via e-mail because she caught me having a Gchat conversation with an ex that had started because of a Facebook status. So it's a little different for us.

We can't sit in one place and have a conversation with someone without wondering if something is or isn't happening *somewhere else*. We want more; there is always something else, something better *out there*. Many of us feel less secure in our relationships and friendships, even with friends we communicate with on a regular basis. We feel lonely, despite keeping in touch.

Our generation has spent roughly half our lives without these gadgets and apps, and the other half becoming addicted to and dependent on them. Many of us can dial back to the time none of it existed. We remember our clearer minds, activities, communication styles, and attention spans before the world changed, though sometimes it feels like a faint and distant memory. I, for one, remember the accountability that went along with the absence of cell phones—the absolute requirement that we could not be more than fifteen minutes late to meet someone or they'd think we were rudely standing them up. I remember awkward conversations that had to happen in person or over the phone and the way that living through those difficult moments and knowing I had the ability to speak my mind changed me, made me stronger, more confident, and independent. I remember dinners with friends during which we all paid attention to each other and then spent hours after the meal together, without one of us leaving because we had made plans on our smartphones in the interim. I remember privacy and loyalty in relationships and having so much to talk about at the end of the day because we had not spoken since the morning. I remember coping with my feelings by taking the time to contemplate and simply sitting with my own thoughts. I remember Sunday mornings with the paper, reading and discussing articles without distraction, and feeling proud that I knew what was going on in the world. I remember how much easier it was to be loyal without a stream of photos or updates from our exes tempting us to stray, or any means to impulsively text or e-mail. I remember reading a book without distraction and enjoying my life without having the urge to broadcast every detail to everyone else. I remember these things with nostalgia because for me and many others, they have ceased to exist.

2

Generation, Interrupted

One of my best friends—we'll call her Donna—recently sent me an e-mail. The proportions of its craziness both shocked me and felt strangely familiar. She wrote:

> This morning I was waiting for the subway and managed to drop my iPhone onto the tracks. It would have been run over by a train. I panicked! Without hesitation, I jumped onto the tracks to retrieve it. Two very nice men pulled me back up. Everyone on the platform thought I was pulling an Anna Karenina. So embarrassing. I was waiting for the express, but the local came first and I boarded immediately.

Anyone who's lived in New York City knows never to wait near the edge of the subway platform for fear of falling onto the tracks (or getting pushed by a random luna-tic). My friend grew up in the city and is well aware of this rule. Nevertheless, this responsible twenty-nine-year-old, the same twenty-nine-year-old who got a near-perfect score on her SATs and went to Princeton, risked her life and vol-untarily *jumped onto* the subway tracks, just to save her iPhone. A piece of *plastic*.

The rational part of me says: I can't believe that we are so desperate to hold on to our phones that we'd put ourselves in danger. But the truth is I'm pretty sure that if this same friend dropped her iPhone onto the subway tracks tomor-row, she wouldn't hesitate to attempt this feat again. And neither would I.

I think about the many times I wasn't able to tear myself away from my phone to pay attention to the person right in front of me. Or all the times a person right in front of me has been too busy calling, texting, e-mailing, tweeting, and updating a status to give me the time of day. A year ago, I was working rather late on this very book. I was trying to reword an anecdote, and I asked my wife to help me. She said, "Hmm," and looked down for a while. I assumed she was thinking about it, mulling over all of the different ways she could help my poor anecdote. About ten minutes later, I became skeptical. This seemed like an inordinate amount of time to be thinking. I leaned over and realized that she was playing Candy Crush. Not only was she playing the game, but she was buying more lives, which meant she had played at least three rounds in the previous twenty minutes. I was alarmed and exclaimed that I thought she was helping me with my book! Her response was that she had received an e-mail, checked it, responded, and then had forgotten about helping me and decided to start up a game of Candy Crush. The fact is, I can't blame her. I spent an hour this morning trying to beat Level 287 in Candy Crush instead of finishing this chapter (btw, I'm really proud of being on Level 287). And even as I sit here now attempting to write, my father is sending me repeated FaceTime requests that come directly to my computer. He thinks it's funny to FaceTime when he is fifteen feet away from me.

About six months ago, a friend called me to ask me for job advice. She called my work line early in the morning (which is never a good plan if you want my full attention, because it means that I have my iPhone fully in front of me while I talk on the landline). She was deciding between staying in her job at a prominent advertising company or leaving and opening up her own agency (which she absolutely did not have enough experience or connections to do). At around minute seven of the conversation, I became immersed in my iPhone on a group text discussing the affair one of our friends was having with another (far more juicy than the job hunt!) and I found myself making the unavoidable and totally distracted "Oh yeah, that's amazing" and "Yeah, definitely" and "Wow . . . Wow . . ." comments that are code for "I AM NOT PAYING ATTENTION." Before I knew it, my friend had said, "You know what, you're right. Okay, I gotta go. I love you!" and gotten off the phone. I assume it was the "Yeah, definitely" default that gave her the justification to and confirmation that she should quit her job and start her own company. Which is exactly what she did. Sadly, she did not have much luck (which I could have told her would happen had I been listening!) and she closed down her agency within a year, couldn't find a job, and went to business school. Oh well.

It never feels good to know that you aren't being a good friend. The guilt always surfaces once you see how annoyed your friend is when you leave them for the night. Afterward, you think, *Oh God, I shouldn't have checked my phone in the middle of that*—but at the time, you see the text notification or hear the irresistible chime of a new e-mail and your hand reaches for the phone before you even realize you're doing it.

In informal surveys of my friends and colleagues, one out of every two people I talked to check their phones immediately after sex, and almost 10 percent check their phones *in the middle of the act*. The smartphone has become the modern post-sex cigarette, no less addictive and far more irresistible.

I speak from experience. I've been known to check my phone immediately after going to bed with someone—and there were definitely a few instances when I heard it buzz or saw the notification pop up and interrupted *whatever* I was doing to check it. Like most people, I wasn't even waiting for any particular message; it was just to relieve the anxiety I feel after a period of time when I haven't checked my phone. I can recall a particular time four or five years ago when I was "in the act" and suddenly saw my iPhone light up. I saw a small green box, which meant it was a text message—much more thrilling than the blue box (e-mail), beige box (Instagram), or orange box (Twitter). My ex-girlfriend happened to see it too and knew me too well. "You have to be kidding me" were the words I think I got (by the way, not words you want to hear "in the act" for any reason whatsoever). I tried to force the argument that she had already ruined the moment so I might as well just check the phone. That didn't work. She went the dramatic route and exclaimed that if I checked it, it would show how truly *NOT* devoted I was to our relationship (ah, women . . .). I weighed my options. And then something miraculous happened. Her phone, next to mine, also lit up. It was green. Like two cowboys (cowgirls?) walking into opposite sides of the local bar, we stared at each other. Who would make the first move? Suddenly we were on an equal playing field. "Why are you looking at me like that? I'm not going to answer it!" she said. I was back to being the loser who couldn't resist. At this point, it was clear that the night from *that* angle was over. So I reached over and checked my phone. *CNN Breaking News—Samsung unveils the Galaxy Smartphone on Verizon.* Are you kidding me? I looked over at my girlfriend. She was texting back her ex-girlfriend who had happened to text her that she would be coming into town the next day. Man, I really lost that one.

My girlfriend eventually decided that neither of us was allowed to check our phones until fifteen minutes after getting out of bed, which was a great rule that I followed . . . for about six months. We just couldn't help ourselves. I don't know any two people who currently wait the fifteen minutes. I've asked around. From when I started writing this book three years ago through today, there has been a marked acceleration of our addiction and thus a marked decrease in our free time. Fifteen minutes? I haven't had fifteen minutes to just sit and enjoy something since 2007. It just doesn't happen. That said, I still think it's a good idea, if you can do it, because looking at a phone so intensely interrupts that afterglow and the bonding time two people should share. That is the cheesiest sentence you'll find in this book, I promise. But it's true! Far too often we surrender moments we should have together to check our phones. We simply can't stop.

Some time ago, I took my now-ex-girlfriend Gina on a four-day trip to a spa for her thirtieth birthday. I figured that an escape to a far-off and deserted place replete with professional massage therapists, bottles of wine, and so-called Japanese soaking tubs would be a welcome and necessary respite.

After boarding the plane and suffering a momentary panic attack when I thought the in-flight Wi-Fi wasn't working, I was relieved when I saw "Gogo Inflight" available in the wireless network list. I was finally ready to start relaxing, my iPad, iPhone, chargers, and USB cords in hand.

Forty minutes into a game of wireless Uno with someone named "ManOfTheMountain" from Pyongyang—how anyone managed to get an iPad or iPhone into North Korea and commence a game of wireless Uno I will never know—I felt someone tapping my shoulder. Apparently, Gina had been saying my name repeatedly for two minutes, but I had been so focused on my game, and the music coming from my Pandora app was so loud, that I hadn't heard her.

"I have an idea for this weekend," she said.

"What?" I asked, expecting her to suggest activities like couple's massages, dinner in town, or tennis—all acceptable options from my point of view.

"I think we should make this a technology-free trip. No iPhones, iPads, Gchatting, or e-mailing. Let's just hang out and reconnect and forget the outside world." Oh no . . . I felt a jolt of worry. This idea was *not* acceptable.

But after taking a deep breath, I had to admit that the idea was actually quite sweet, thoughtful, and definitely novel considering the world we lived in—and considering it was me she was talking to. This was her birthday trip, so I agreed to the plan. I hoped I could do it, but history and my gut told me otherwise. (I had done my cleanse a few months before but had quickly reverted to my junkie ways.) Almost immediately, a wave of unease swept over me. I looked down at my phone the way a fisherman might look at his wife (or husband) right before setting off on a three-week sail and stuttered what I knew was probably a lie: "Y-yeah. Sounds awesome, I'm down." I then proceeded to do a mental run-through of our vacation schedule, looking for potential moments—massages, manicures, getting dressed—when Gina would be busy so I could quickly "reconnect" with my technological devices.

And over the next four days, reconnect I did. I pretended to be reading a book or the *New York Times* on my iPad when I was really using Gchat with friends I would be seeing in two days. I tried to wear outfits with pockets so that I could sneakily bring my phone to the bathroom to get a few texts in during dinners and lunch by the pool. It turns out that 90 degree weather is not conducive to hiding digital devices. Perhaps most embarrassingly, I connected headphones to my iPhone and covered it so I could pretend I was just listening to music, turning my back and typing any moment I could. It was pathetic.

I felt bad that I wasn't being honest with Gina, but I felt guilty so much of the time that I'd become almost immune to it. I'd given up trying to change. Part of me didn't even care—I was just obsessing about when I could use my devices again. On the last day of the trip, Gina asked me if I could please at least stop plugging earphones into my iPhone as she was aware in the perfect silence of the spa that there was no music coming out of them. She had known the whole time. She had given up on me. But this was okay—I had given up on myself years ago. I was an addict. The least I could do was accept it.

Sure, it can make me feel depressed and anxious, and I live with a near-constant state of guilt because of it, but I will always go back to it, no matter what.

I wanted to know if others felt the same way. I asked hundreds of people to describe their relationship with their smartphone. They used words like *addicted*, *love/hate*, *dependent*, *marriage*, *lifeline*, *wife*—and even *tortured*, *chained*, and *captive*. In fact, almost 80 percent of those who responded used these types of negative, obsessive words, compared to only 20 percent who used positive words like *practical* and *useful*. A few said that they had given up their iPhones and felt more free *without* them, only to buy them again later because they felt they were "missing out" on too much.

I found it heartening in a way to know I was far from the only one who got seriously stressed out when I heard the ping or buzz or triton (or the *Beverly Hills, 90210* ringtone) or any other alert that a message was waiting. Most people talked about the anxiety and frustration they feel because of their ever-present need to check. One person said, "I need to get rid of the message notification immediately," while another described it as "incredibly frustrating, to the point of madness." There were, of course, some extremes, such as the person who said, "[Text messages and Instagram notifications] make me feel really antsy, like when I'm the last person in a store before it closes. Also it kind of makes me feel like I need to pee." Another said, "The waiting message makes me feel fanatical. It is gut-wrenching." Overall, out of more than two hundred people in my informal poll, more than 60 percent used words like *anxiety*, *stress*, and *frustration* to describe their physical and mental reactions when they know a message is waiting for them. And yet we can't even fathom giving up our phones.

. . .

Some people use specific time frames to discuss their child's developmental stages; I use them to describe the trajectory of my smartphone addiction. When I switched from my PalmPilot to a BlackBerry, I felt like my life was finally going somewhere. When I finally switched from a BlackBerry to an iPhone, it felt like the dawn of a new era. And every time I upgrade my iPhone, I feel as though I have a new lease on life. About 90 percent of my decision to switch from a Black-Berry to an iPhone a few years ago was based on my inability to function as a healthy and focused human being when the red light on my BlackBerry was blinking. I know that I could have simply turned off the notification function that many of us refer to as the "blinking red light"—in fact, I did that three times, only to turn the light *back on* less than a week later because I couldn't stand not to know when messages came in, and without it I was checking my phone even more. A friend who also recently switched to the iPhone told me that getting rid of the blinking red light was also one of her main reasons for tossing her BlackBerry—because she had become like Pavlov's dog. "I would see that blinking light out of the corner of my eye and it haunted me," she said. "I saw the light blinking when it wasn't even blinking at all." We both thought switching to an iPhone would help. I fooled myself into thinking I would feel differently as long as there wasn't a blinking red light. I soon learned that there is a very underused function on an iPhone that alerts you with three quick flashes (like lightning!) whenever you have a new message. (For those of you who want to further complicate and accentuate your addictions, go to Settings> General>Accessibility>LED Flash for Alerts. You're welcome. I'm sorry.) It's the brightest light I've ever seen. After having it on for a few months, I began feeling as though I was experiencing the beginning of a seizure every time I got an e-mail, text, or notification. For my own health and peace of mind, I turned off the LED. Unfortunately, this did not stop me from still being tortured by the pop-up messages.

It's no wonder we start twitching when we get any sort of electronic notification, because, like Pavlov's dog, our brains have been rewired. When we experience something pleasurable, a neurotransmitter called dopamine is released in our system, giving us a euphoric feeling, which our brains will want to re-create. According to Gary Small, MD, "the same neural pathways . . . that reinforce dependence on substances can reinforce compulsive technology behaviors that are just as addictive and potentially destructive." We start to crave whatever made us feel that way, whether it's an actual drug, like nicotine, or that someone "liked" our photo on Instagram, sent us a funny or loving text, liked our event on Facebook, or tweeted at us. In a *Psychology Today* article, Dr. Small explains that nonaddicts also feel the dopamine effect, because it is so powerful. In fact, too many of us have become compulsive enough that some in the psychiatric community have started to wonder if Internet Compulsion Disorder—the name writer Bill Davidow has bestowed upon this national epidemic—should be included in the new *Diagnostic and Statistical Manual of Mental Disorders* (*DSM*). This new addiction is a worldwide phenomenon: the tech giant Cisco surveyed members of Gen Y—that is, eighteen-to-thirty-year-olds—in eighteen countries and found that 60 percent check their phones compulsively, 90 percent before they get out of bed. I would argue this number is closer to 100 percent, as I haven't seen someone get out of bed without first checking their smartphone in at least seven years. Keane Angle, a digital strategist at 360i, a digital marketing agency in New York, believes that the desire to check our smartphones has become "a basic human need—the need for acceptance and affirmation of personal worth. When you get an e-mail, a tweet, or a 'like' on one of your status updates, it's like the crack version of a compliment—it's bite-sized, its effects last only a few seconds, and it's highly addictive."

James E. Katz, the director of emerging media studies at Boston University, explained that the fact that we *don't know* what news we may receive is what aggravates this compulsive need to check. And yet, he considers "the constant checking [to be] an exercise in optimism . . . Eternal hope delivered in tiny bits." I like Katz's positive spin on this addiction. I know the message could be anything—and despite my anxiety, I often think my buzzing phone will deliver great news. Unless you have a job where every text or e-mail makes you miserable, I think many people feel this sense of expectation. It's always exciting to know that something is waiting for you, that there is a flutter of possibility.

We need to satisfy this craving so much, some experts are saying, that in doing so we are acquiring a new type of attention deficit disorder—one combined with an Internet addiction—and many in the field are worried. In an interview with the *New York Times*, Dr. John Ratey, a clinical associate professor of psychiatry at Harvard, used the term *acquired attention deficit disorder* to describe those whose brains are "accustomed to a constant stream of digital stimulation and feel bored in the absence of it." The digital stimulation could be from anything: television, Internet, social media, or smartphones. And Dr. Elias Aboujaoude, who helped lead a study on problematic Internet use, argues that there is a marked link between Internet addiction and attention deficit disorder. He says, "The more we become used to just sound bites and tweets, the less patient we will be with more complex, more meaningful information." In his comprehensive and entertaining book *Virtually You*, Aboujaoude describes a study that was conducted in 2008 among 752 school-age children in South Korea, where a third of the students who had been diagnosed with ADHD were considered "addicted" to the Internet. Just as striking, Aboujaoude notes a 2004 study of college students in Taiwan found that 32 percent of Internet addicts had ADHD, whereas only 8 percent of non-Internet addicts had ADHD. While it's outside of the realm of my authority to untangle the causal relationship between Internet addiction and ADHD, it's true that psychologists and studiers of the *DSM* would argue that Internet addiction cannot cause ADHD and that an "acquired" attention deficit disorder is not a real possibility. I'm inclined to agree with them though I do think that ADHD-like traits seem to be increasingly present in Internet and smartphone addicts. I certainly experience them.

Experts' concerns have only grown in recent years, particularly with the advent of smartphones—so much so that Larry D. Rosen, PhD, an international expert in what he calls the "psychology of technology," believes we are *all* headed for what he calls an iDisorder. In an article for Lifehack.org about his book *iDisorder: Understanding Our*

Obsession with Technology and Overcoming Its Hold on Us, he writes that we will all "exhibit signs and symptoms of a psychiatric disorder such as OCD, narcissism, addiction or even ADHD, which are manifested through [our] use—or overuse—of technology." Harvard's Ratey explains that our brains are consistently "hijacked" by all this media—and that when we absentmindedly reach for our phones or can't resist the urge to grab our devices, we are like drug addicts. "Drug addicts don't think; they just start moving. Like moving for your BlackBerry" or your iPhone.

My friend Dr. Amy Wicker told me about a simple self-test that has proven accurate in identifying problems with alcohol known as the CAGE questionnaire, utilized by health care professionals to see if a patient may be addicted to alcohol. *CAGE* stands for *cut*, *annoy*, *guilty*, and *eye-opener*, each of which is represented in the questionnaire. Dr. Wicker told me that if you answer yes to at least two of these questions, the possibility of alcoholism should be investigated further. I began to wonder if the CAGE questionnaire could be used to determine usage patterns that reflect problems with excessive smartphone use with similar levels of accuracy.

Have you ever felt you should Cut down on your usage?

To help you, here are some telltale signs from my own life:

- Your friends constantly make sarcastic comments about your smartphone or Facebook use and say things like "Look at Kim on her iPhone again! She's so much fun to have dinner with!" I've gotten this one hundreds of times.

- You've made life-changing decisions because of your addiction (e.g., you failed to go to class because you were immersed in heavy stalking of your ex, or perhaps you called in sick to work because you drunk-texted a coworker the night before and simply could not stand to be seen).

Have you ever been <u>A</u>nnoyed by your friends' criticism of your addiction?

Again, use my own experiences as a guide:

- Your friends tell you in advance that they will only go to dinner with you if you keep your smartphone in your bag and away from the table. In response, you get defensive and threaten to call the dinner off.
- Your friends grab your phone out of your hand while you are texting in an effort to express their annoyance and, in turn, you grab theirs out of their bag and throw them on the floor.

Have you ever felt <u>G</u>uilty or bad about your usage?

These are particularly embarrassing for me:

- You have started faking bathroom trips during dinners to get your fix without people knowing about it because you feel guilty.
- You find yourself lying about your usage to almost everyone you know.
- You write an entire book about it (ugh).

Do you ever need to check your smartphone first thing in the morning (an <u>E</u>ye-opener) in order to start your day and steady your nerves?

45

Things to admit to yourself:

- You cannot go more than ten minutes (one minute) after you wake up without checking your smartphone/social media.
- Not seeing your phone on your bedside in the morning sends you into a state of complete anxiety. You jump out of bed, find your laptop, and use the Find My iPhone app to create loud pings to see if you can find it. If that doesn't work, you begin blaming others. Someone must have stolen it! Later, you find it in the bathroom.

When I used the CAGE questions as a guide to talk to people in my generation about their smartphone and Internet use, I estimated that 96 percent of us were addicted. The language we used to talk about our digital lives was strikingly similar to the words used by other friends and people I've spoken to who have gone through actual substance abuse. Our lives are full of shame and secrecy. One person admitted, "I try to hide from my boyfriend the fact that when I wake up each morning, I roll over and check my Facebook and Instagram, and pretend that I am really just on my side taking a vitamin and drinking water." Also, do people really keep vitamins by their bedside? All I have are my phone/iPad/computer and their respective chargers.

William Powers, author of *Hamlet's BlackBerry*, describes our addiction as akin to being on a "hamster wheel" of always needing another hit of dopamine. He said to me, "There is something satisfying that we all feel deep inside when we hear the sound of a new e-mail coming in or see that . . . light on our phones. But really, how satisfying is it? How much is that micro-feeling adding to your life versus what you are giving up by dividing your attention?"

• • •

Media, television networks, and even some schools are finding that their only choice is to play into our acquired attention deficit disordered brains and create shorter programming, send out constant reminders about school-related events on websites and Twitter pages, and write countless blog posts in order to reach this new type of increasingly addled mind.

The media has been equally affected. I remember writing two-hundred-fifty-word articles for the *MTV News* website and being asked to cut them down to just one hundred or one hundred twenty-five words because our audience would get bored and click away. (Thank God; it became outrageously tiring to find two hundred fifty words to say about Miley—this of course was before her 2013 *VMA* "performance.") In one year, the suggested word count went down to seventy-five or even *fifty*—barely enough words to convey anything remotely journalistic beyond a bulleted list of comments and a joke or two.

The constant distractions and all our time online are clearly affecting our brains and may even be leading to new challenges in learning. Matt Richtel's 2010 *New York Times* article "Growing Up Digital, Wired for Distraction" featured a group of bright kids who were failing many of their classes because they did not have the attention span to finish the assignments, and in some cases even forgot to do homework. They were consistently plugged in—surfing the Web, texting, playing video games—and younger brains, which are still developing, get used to this behavior. Richtel wrote, "'Their brains are rewarded not for staying on task but for jumping to the next thing,' said Michael Rich, an associate professor at Harvard Medical School and executive director of the Center on Media and Child Health in Boston." Dr. Rich and other experts are worried that staring at screens will rewire kids' brains, with harmful and lasting effects. Teachers are concerned that their students can't concentrate at all and that they are leaving high school with less-than-ideal reading, writing, and discussion skills. Some teachers are resorting to reading books aloud in class because students can't focus long enough to read twenty pages of a chapter at night.

These detrimental effects are more obvious in developing brains but can be seen in adult brains as well. Nonstop distraction hinders productivity. According to a 2011 study by Cisco, 24 percent of college students and young professionals "experience three to five interruptions in a given hour, while 84 percent get interrupted at least once while trying to complete a project." Further, a recent study of university students found that those who multitasked heavily in a variety of media—texting, instant messaging, Facebooking, and tweeting while at work or a social gathering—were less likely to process information in a meaningful way. They had slower response times, were more easily distracted by irrelevant information, were unable to switch tasks easily, and retained useless information in their short-term memory. In other words, they may not have been born with ADD, but it certainly seems as though they *acquired* it.

Perhaps we were never meant to multitask. After all, according to the aforementioned study of university students, "processing multiple incoming streams of information is considered a challenge for human cognition." Further, psychiatrist and author Edward M. Hallowell describes multitasking as a "mythical activity in which people believe they can perform two or more tasks simultaneously as effectively as one." It's why your mom told you to turn off the TV while doing your homework, why some companies are now preventing their employees from using some social media sites, and why people have died while texting and driving. As Dr. Richard Cytowic explains on his *Fallible Mind* blog, "The same inefficiency that freezes up your computer bogs down a brain when it is forced to divide attention among multiple tasks . . . In a world of nonstop distraction, you may be able to juggle things for a while, but you can't keep it up; it simply takes more energy and bandwidth than we have."

Never giving our brains a break is dangerous; according to the *New York Times* article by Matt Richtel, scientists in California found that rats were only able to develop permanent or long-lasting memories after experiencing something new if they *rested*. No one likes to be compared to a rodent, but we all need to power down in order to process our experiences in a valuable way, to retain what we have learned and establish the memory. Other research shows that taking a quick rest will actually *enhance* our memory. As reported in *Psychological Science*, two groups of individuals listened to a story, after which one group played a video game and another shut their eyes for about ten minutes. The study found that "memory can be boosted by taking a brief 'wakeful rest' after learning something verbally new and that memory lasts not just immediately but over a longer term." Apparently, whatever we do in the short time after we learn something new will determine the quality of our memory. We don't necessarily need to take a nap—we just need to take a break from all the noise. We need more Thoreau-inspired experiences. We need to find our own Waldens. A University of Michigan study revealed that walking in nature helped people learn more effectively than walking through a busy urban environment, which may mean that our brains get fatigued from an onslaught of information. I can tell which chapters of this book I wrote at my apartment in New York City versus the ones I wrote out in the country at my parents' house. I notice that I have a harder time finding my voice in the chapters written in the oversaturated and bustling city. You'll probably notice too. Being in the silence of the country allows me to relax just enough so that I actually absorb what I am writing and how it sounds. This type of downtime is essential for our brains to work better, but in a constant state of stimulation, we're not allowing ourselves to have it.

In addition to making us less responsive to people we love and perhaps a bit dumber, our addiction also makes us do some pretty crazy things. Thirty percent of people I talked to seemed alarmed when reading a sentence in which the word *BlackBerry* referred to a fruit, almost half the people know how to drive with their knees so that they can text and drive, and just over 20 percent admitted to only buying fingerless gloves because it's too hard to text while wearing regular gloves or mittens. One Christmas, I actually cut the fingers off a beautiful pair of cashmere gloves my mother bought me so that I could freely type on my phone during my wintertime commute. I am still disturbed by this, though apparently I'm not disturbed enough to have refrained from specifically asking my parents for fingerless gloves the following Christmas.

I am admittedly one of those people who tend to lose things easily and frequently. This year, I made the decision to attach an adhesive pocket to the back of my iPhone to serve as a wallet. I may lose my wallet five times in a year, but it's almost impossible to lose something that I'm checking every two to three minutes, so I finally arrived at the brilliant idea that if I actually turn my iPhone into a wallet, I won't lose anything. My iPhone has functioned as my wallet for over a year now and I have yet to cancel any cards or take that arduous trip to the DMV to replace my license.

A few years ago, I sat on a panel at South by Southwest about teenage cell phone use in America. When one of the speakers mentioned that he missed the good ol' days when people used to put down their phones during dinner and pay attention to their friends instead of texting or scrolling through Facebook, the room lit up with excited nods and chants of "Yes!" The audience included smartphone addicts like me, bloggers, and digital media professionals—basically all the kinds of people who annoy you at dinner because they can't put down their devices. Yet all of us were agreeing enthusiastically that we hated how much our dinner companions and friends constantly ignored *us*. I wondered if some of the people nodding in staunch agreement were sort of guiltily admitting that they are often the ones who are too busy tweeting, Instagramming, e-mailing, Tumblring, Facebooking, BBMing, or Snapchatting to give their friends and family the attention they deserve—I know I was.

We hate ourselves for using these things so much, but we learn to live with the guilt—we are *relieved* instead of aggravated or insulted when others take out their phones at dinner, because it means we can too. It's like when you want to cancel plans with someone but are dreading that awkward e-mail and then they send you a text canceling before you have the chance to! The best. That is how I feel when I see a friend take out her phone at dinner. What a relief. I can now reach for mine. We can remember when we were focused and attentive, and it bothers us, but that doesn't mean we will stop.

While on the panel, I began to notice how the reactions differed throughout the audience. The group consisted mainly of people in my age group, between twenty-five and thirty-five, but there were also several teenagers, as well as a few people who were at least forty or fifty. When the complaints about tech and smartphone addiction were raised, those in their midtwenties and early thirties were by far the most passionate—responding as if we were all inmates of the same prison, aware of our lives beforehand, and dumbfounded by how we had let ourselves become captive to these devices that now run our lives. In contrast, the younger members of the audience seemed less annoyed and at times almost nonchalant and generally unaffected. I guess it makes sense if you consider that these digital natives haven't known life any other way. But what really surprised me was that the older people in the room, those who had spent much more time in their lives *without* such technology, were just as affected by its hypnotizing pull.

I guess I shouldn't have been surprised. Of all the people I talked into joining Foursquare (my parents, seven friends, and two coworkers), my *dad* was the one who became the most addicted. Foursquare is the location-based social media game that crowns a person "mayor" of any location once they have visited and "checked in" at a place more than anyone else. It works with your phone's GPS functionality, so you need to actually be at or very near the place at which you are requesting to "check in." When someone checks in more than you, Foursquare sends you an e-mail saying that you've been "ousted" as the mayor. The other day I was ousted from my mayorship of the Amanpulo resort in the Philippines. It destroys me that I will likely never get it back and there is nothing I can do about it.

My father is a retired Wall Street sales trader with a serious competitive streak. He and my mother are happily married and live in Bridgehampton. They have the kind of connected relationship and home life I aspire to emulate. Nonetheless, thanks to Foursquare, he became wildly obsessed with becoming mayor of as many places in the Hamptons as possible. Most days he would wake up around six A.M. to play a round of golf, then drive through town, checking into Bobby Van's, Candy Kitchen, Starbucks, Hampton Coffee Company (yes, that's *two* coffee places), Pierre's, and the bank, in addition to any other place he actually needed to be. He even became mayor of long-term parking at JFK International Airport for two months. He felt particularly proud of this mayorship. I think my favorite aspect of my father's Foursquare addiction, however, was immediately after he realized that one of the perks of being the mayor of certain locations, like Starbucks, was that you got special deals. At Bridgehampton Starbucks, my dad learned, his mayorship granted him one free coffee per day. He would strut into Starbucks, order coffee at the counter, and when the cashier asked him to pay, he would whip out his phone, say something weird like "not so fast," and flash his Foursquare deal for them, winning his free coffee. It was out of a *Seinfeld* or *Curb Your Enthusiasm* episode. He had gamed the system. He had won.

My mom and I weren't concerned about this new obsession; we were more amused—this was so in line with my dad's personality and we enjoyed teasing him about it. When I visited my parents shortly after introducing my father to the game, he took over our dinner conversation, venting his frustration that someone named "Ian Z." was still mayor of Bobby Van's. My dad just couldn't seem to steal the mayoral title, even though he checked in at least *three* times a day. The day he finally became mayor was great: We had steak to celebrate, and Ian Z. sent my dad a friend request on Foursquare—maybe out of respect or maybe out of pure curiosity. Ian Z. must have felt the same way that Andre Agassi felt when Pete Sampras beat him: completely floored and humble and exhilarated. I thought that with this victory, my father's tenth virtual mayoral title, his obsession would die down. I was wrong.

The next week, my father went to work out at the gym, where he was the mayor and was always greeted with open arms by its staff, who couldn't seem to understand why a man who went to the gym only four times a week was mayor while they, who went every day, were not. Clearly they had no idea about his late-night and early-morning drive-bys. In any case, thirty minutes into the session, my dad's trainer said, "Ray, I gotta ask you a question."

My father, unsuspecting, said, "What's up?"

"Well, the other day, I was heading into Citarella in Bridgehampton and I saw you drive into the parking lot, stop for about forty-five seconds, then pull out again and drive away. You weren't checking in on Foursquare, were you? Because you know that's cheating."

My dad swore to quit Foursquare on the spot—well, as soon as he had stolen the last mayoral title (for Bridge-hampton Cemetery—who wants to be mayor of dead people?) from his archnemesis, Ian Z. On, November 2, 2010, my father became the mayor of the cemetery, and he quit Foursquare the next day. Even though I was happy he had the strength to quit, I was also helplessly and absurdly proud that my own dad had become the virtual mayor of all the restaurants and most of the bars I went to in the Hamptons.

Foursquare and its virtual victory quest took over many of my loved ones' lives for a period, not just my dad's. A few of my friends would go out at night even when they didn't want to, just so they could check into places and re-instate their mayorships, or would travel miles out of the way just to get new Foursquare "badges." If we were a few visits away from becoming mayor, we would aim to go to a specific part of town just to check into whatever bar, hotel, or restaurant we wanted to be mayor of. Sometimes it was for bragging rights; other times there were incentives, like prizes that were blatant marketing ploys. We were addicted to the faux connection, to the distraction.

Just like Friendster and Myspace before it, many think Foursquare is quickly becoming irrelevant. Now that people can link their Instagram and Foursquare accounts and tag locations on their photographs, there is little reason to sign directly into the Foursquare application. Like many of its predecessors and many that will follow, Foursquare was meaningless, pointless, and completely addictive while it lasted. But like many of its peers, it has died down and may become obsolete, paving the way for the newer, shinier so-cial media like Instagram, Tinder, and Snapchat. One day, those will be rendered obsolete as well when we find some-thing else we love more tomorrow, chasing it down onto the subway tracks.

3

Facebook Is Ruining My Life

As I was reading *Walden* and reacquainting myself with Henry David Thoreau's thoughts on the joys of solitude, I tried to remember the last time I'd spent any time by myself—truly by myself, with only my thoughts to occupy my mind, no iPhone or iPad or computer to distract me.

I thought about the time right after Samantha, my long-term girlfriend, broke up with me, and how I had done *everything* possible to avoid confronting my feelings. The healthy reaction would have been to sit by myself and reflect, as I had in high school or the beginning of college when going through other difficult times. But instead of dealing with how I felt, I self-medicated by staying constantly connected: over the course of ten days I e-mailed all of my friends, signed on to Gchat, texted, tweeted, FaceTimed, and checked Facebook hundreds, perhaps thousands of times.

What had seemed like a blessing of distraction was a curse in disguise. I realized that I had not experienced anything like Thoreau's idea of solitude in six years—since I first got a smartphone.

Alone time is a chance to contemplate what's going on in my life or where I am mentally or emotionally. It's a time to figure things out, when no third parties are interrupting or hijacking my thoughts. I think I used to be more secure when there was more bandwidth for alone time. Spending time with just me made me *like* me more. I got to know myself better, and so I would know how best to handle challenges, disagreements, and times of strife. The more time I spent anxiously typing away on my smartphone and being my virtual self on social media, the less close I felt to my core, the part of me that made the best decisions, the part of me that was truly the best I could be. I always loved Thoreau's words "I have a great deal of company in my house; especially in the morning when nobody calls." Thoreau was not a hermit, he just understood the importance of a divide between oneself and the world at large. "Individuals, like nations, must have suitable broad and natural boundaries," he wrote. He complained once about a friendship, saying, "We meet at very short intervals, not having had time to acquire any new value for each other." Sounds familiar. Everyone we've ever met in our lives is just a click away, and if we don't want to think about something difficult, we can text; write an e-mail; check Facebook, Snapchat, Instagram; scour YouTube; play a video game; make plans—we don't have to be alone if we don't want to be. True solitude has become uncomfortable for us.

It's been said that Thoreau was the most content man alive because he had found the balance and stability in total solitude. The ultimate transcendentalist—he believed in the goodness of man and nature—Thoreau lived a life without distraction (granted, this was 1845, long before the phonograph or the telephone) in natural surroundings next to Walden Pond in Massachusetts. Before Thoreau, many famous theorists and great religious figures sat in seclusion in order to connect with and speak to their spirit guides; the prophets, sadhus, and yogis conducted their visionary experiences and trances in the desert, a cave, or some other place that allowed for absolute solitude.

Ralph Waldo Emerson, another transcendentalist, described how being alone could bring you a deeper appreciation of friends and society: "The soul environs itself with friends, that it may enter into a grander self-acquaintance or solitude; and it goes alone, for a season, that it may exalt its conversation or society." Emerson believed in friendship, but he also valued solitude. We need our alone time in order to be functional and emotionally aware in our relationships, at work, and in friendships; that is how we can become better people and be introspective, self-analytical, and reflective—all those things that make us *human*.

An emerging body of research in the field of clinical psychology suggests that we should be spending more quality time alone. In an article titled "The Power of Lonely: What

We Do Better Without Other People Around," Leon Ney-fakh states that "spending time alone, if done right, can be good for us—that certain tasks and thought processes that are best carried out without anyone else around, and even the most socially motivated among us should regularly be taking time to ourselves if we want to have fully developed personalities and be capable of focus and creative think-ing." Proponents of solitude claim that if we want to get the most out of the time we spend with other people, we need to spend certain time *away* from them too. The ol' saying "Absence makes the heart grow fonder" is more deeply true than any of us completely understood.

Still, many of us go to great extremes to ensure that we will not be alone with our thoughts. I remember when I was in high school, taking breaks from homework or walk-ing to school and noticing the world around me. I went to Brearley, widely considered one of the top high schools in the nation, and while I credit my teachers, curriculum, and peers with the fantastic education I received, I think the time I spent alone in high school helped too. I had time to reflect and to absorb the information of the day. By the time college started, I was immersed in my phone and soon would be immersed in Friendster (RIP), Myspace, and Face-book. I don't think I truly needed study breaks in college, as I only studied for five or six minutes at a time between checking my phone or Facebook. In high school, I remem-ber sitting at my desk for six or seven hours, sometimes, without a single distraction. Today, I've barely opened my eyes and I'm on my phone; my iPhone reigns.

There are now over 1.15 billion active Facebook users. The latest numbers on Twitter indicate that it has over 240 million monthly active users. Nielsen found that between 2003 and 2009, the total time spent on social networking sites went up *883 percent* among all ages, with teens between thirteen and seventeen years old increasing their usage 256 percent in one year, "growing at a rate faster than any other age group." They also found that the average teenager sends and receives more than seven text messages for *every hour* they are awake. Teenage girls send and receive about four thousand texts a month.

If we assume it takes thirty seconds to read a text message, think of a response, and type a reply, then we can deduce that based on the numbers of texts they send, the average teenager or twentysomething spends roughly an hour to an hour and ten minutes of their waking hours each day texting. If we add to that (at least) three or four hours of time on Instagram, Snapchat, Facebook, Twitter, Tumblr, Pinterest, and similar member-community sites—Common Sense Media found that 25 percent of teens log on to their favorite social networking site more than ten times a day— we arrive at an average of *at least* four to five hours of electronic and social media communication per day. Combined with school, after-school jobs, socializing with friends, and hopefully a tech-free dinner once in a while, this number leaves the average young person with virtually no time to be alone with their thoughts.

But it's not just connection-crazed teens who are affected. All of us are spending more and more time in the digital world. Fifty percent of those I spoke with said they spend more than three hours on Facebook or Instagram per day, one out of ten said that they check Facebook, Instagram, or Twitter more than *thirty* times a day, and 61 percent confessed to checking these sites more than five times a day. According to Nielsen's *State of the Media* report, Americans in general spent a total of 53.5 *billion* minutes on Facebook over the course of 2011. It doesn't take a social scientist to deduce that these studies dramatically underestimate the frequency with which we are on social media and our smartphones. Just look around. I'm looking around right now. It's gorgeous outside but my parents' living room could easily be mistaken for an Apple Store. My father sits with his iPhone resting on his leg while he plays Hearts online on his iPad. My wife is to the right, scrolling through Instagram for what I'm counting as the sixth time today. My mom, sitting to my left, is checking Facebook on her iPad while playing Words with Friends on her iPhone. And I'm on my MacBook Air writing about technology and social media changing our lives. I've left my iPhone in the other room but have just discovered that I can text from my iMessage app on my computer, so behind this MS Word window is iMessage, where I have texted nine friends in the last ten minutes. Oh dear. For me and everyone I know, the frequency increases every single day; if we're working, the Facebook window is always open alongside our e-mail. We're constantly refreshing the Instagram feed on our phones. These studies and polls are always one step behind.

I wonder if staying constantly connected—by way of

our screens—still means we are connecting on a *human* level. By eating up our time, communication devices and social media hinder us from being social on a person-to-person, face-to-face basis. And not only that, they may make us want to interact with people *less*.

A June 2011 Pew Research Center poll found that 13 percent of us are occupied with our phones to "prevent unwanted personal interactions." When we can just click a button to express our thoughts and read those of others, suddenly in-person interfacing seems a lot more annoying. Why spend twenty minutes talking on the phone, tying up your device so you can't also be texting and checking e-mail, when a five-word text or 140-character tweet would suffice? I freely admit to doing things like letting the phone ring to "miss" a call, then waiting to respond with a follow-up text—even if I like the person who is calling! Texting is just so much . . . easier.

But it's not as though everyone is bound to complain—our friends don't want us to call them either! The Pew Internet and American Life Project found that 31 percent of American adults prefer to be contacted by text rather than an old-school phone call, and 55 percent of those who send and receive more than fifty messages a day—most likely avid texters under thirty—say they would rather get a text than a voice call. Our devices and all this software are supposed to *enable* connections between people, but on some level, they seem to be sabotaging the actual human-interaction part of our relationships—and many of us appear to be fine with only *typing at each other*. It's far too annoying to talk on an iPhone because I always miss bits and pieces of conversations as I'm pulling the phone away from my ear to text someone back.

• • •

This screened-in stance is not only changing the nature of our relationships, it's also altering how we treat and react to one other—and perhaps even our ability to feel the very human emotion we call empathy. Evolutionary anthropologist Robin Dunbar explains that "emotional closeness declines by around 15 percent a year in the absence of face-to-face contact" and I have found this to be true to some extent for me and my friends. We feel less guilty "breaking up" or disappearing on someone we meet or chat with online, especially if we have not spent much or any time with them in person. It's easier to ignore people or not reply to their e-mails or texts when we don't hear or see them. We don't imagine them staring into their screens, waiting patiently for a response that may not come for days. We don't have to hear if they are upset. It's easy to forget there is a *person* on the other end if we don't hear a voice.

Once at my former restaurant, the Dalloway, one of our managers forgot to place a tequila order for a Margarita Monday party we were having and had publicized through every aspect of the social media spectrum. We had no tequila. If you can recall any of your experiences at the type of dive bar that is light on the tequila and heavy on the triple sec, you know that kind of margarita leaves much to be desired (and also leaves you with a hangover to end all other hangovers). I was livid. I had colleagues, clients, and friends coming. On the phone, when she called to tell me she had forgotten, I was cold, sure, but I knew I was holding back from saying what I really meant (she was terrible at her job as it was). When we hung up, I immediately found her name in my phone and began to text her. I called her sloppy, lazy, and helpless. I would only say these types of terrible things over text or e-mail, never in person or on the phone. I am not even sure I meant the things I was saying, and when she repeatedly typed back "I'm sorry . . . I'm sorry . . . I'm so sorry," I felt no remorse. The fact that she had a face, feelings, a heart, was the farthest thing from my mind. All I saw was the screen I was typing on, and clicking "send" had no equivalence to actually speaking the words to someone's face. I would never have said those things out loud!

When we are constantly plugged in and our thoughts perpetually interrupted, I wonder if it's not just our minds that are hijacked but our empathy as well. Whenever I have to confront an awkward situation, the people around me all say the same thing: "Just text it." I remember being in high school and being given great advice in the midst of a conflict, which was to drop whatever I was doing, find the person with whom I was in disagreement, and face the situation head-on. Now we can sit home and write an e-mail or text them! Situation solved, until you've lost your friends and everyone hates you.

The manager at the Dalloway had made a mistake and ruined a party, but I had launched a texting campaign against her as though she had set the restaurant on fire. It's easy to escalate when there's a device mediating our interactions. Words are so easy to say when you aren't truly saying them.

Beyond saying things we come to regret and hurting people we don't mean to hurt, the other issue with "electronic daggers" is that they leave a paper trail. Within moments of our conversation, the manager had screenshotted my harsh words, sent it to another manager and three bartenders, and then texted, *What a bitch*. Okay, I had been a bitch, but she was stupid to share that with my employees. All four of them, it turned out, hated her, and screenshotted her screen shot and texted it to me. I did the only thing someone in my generation would do. I screenshotted their screen shot of her screen shot and texted it to her. She quit. I still had no tequila.

In *Psychology Today*, Maia Szalavitz writes about a report based on the answers to a survey on empathy administered to fourteen thousand college students that found empathy had dropped by 40 percent. The report analyzed data recorded over thirty years and measured empathy with certain questions. For instance, compared to students of the late 1970s, students today are less likely to agree with statements such as "I sometimes try to understand my friends better by imagining how things look from their perspective" and "I often have tender, concerned feelings for people less fortunate than me." Szalavitz expressed shock that the students did not bother to alter their answers to even appear more compassionate. "If young people don't even care about seeming uncaring, something is seriously wrong," she writes. But why is this happening? Szalavitz speculates that perhaps it has something to do with all the time we spend with our digital devices. "You can't learn to connect and care if you don't practice these things . . . Though social media is an improvement on passive TV viewing and can sometimes aid real friendships, it is still less rich than face-to-face interaction."

I've found that if I read bad news on a screen (via text or Facebook feed or via other social media), I am not as connected to it emotionally—I may think about it for a moment but then I move on to the next post. In contrast, when someone calls me and tells me the news directly, I can perceive the sadness or panic or whatever emotion they are experiencing in their voice—I *feel* that. Through the veil of a monitor, I don't feel the same kind of compassion. On social media, we are being exposed to so much information all the time that I'm not even sure if we're fully capable of processing it, that we truly feel the compassion we as humans should. I wonder if we are more willing and able to toss relationships aside, especially those that primarily live online.

A couple of years ago, a Swedish girl named Clare approached me with a Facebook message. I usually ignore messages from strangers, but for whatever reason, I answered this one. It could have been because I was bored, between girlfriends, or having a (second) bottle of wine. For whatever reason, I replied. We wrote back and forth, which quickly turned to Gchatting, actual e-mailing, text messaging, and finally, talking on the phone. We were in touch about six or seven times a day, and always before we went to sleep. We video-chatted a few times, and I was convinced that she was every bit as beautiful as her profile photos had implied. It felt like the beginning of a real relationship. Our conversations (online and live) were open and flowed well. It seemed like we were building something. Clare was getting ready to come to New York for an internship with a fashion designer—which she had arranged long before she reached out to me—and I was excited to finally spend time with her face-to-face.

But three weeks before she was set to arrive, I met someone—in person. We started dating and before I knew it, I was making excuses to Clare as to why I was no longer available at the times we used to speak. She began to contact me constantly, trying to find out what was going on. She called, I screened. She wrote, I ignored. She Gchatted, I made myself "invisible." For all intents and purposes, I dropped off the face of the earth. It was far too easy. I know that I would never have been able to ignore Clare if I had met her in person and built a real-life bond with her, but because we had spoken primarily through our technological devices, it felt less wrong to shut her out this way. I know it was rude, but, even though I'm not proud of what I did and still feel guilty when I see her status updates on my feed, it also didn't seem unacceptable.

When we meet someone online, a connection can feel real, but at the same time, we usually feel less obligated to treat someone who's basically a string of texts and videos and pictures with respect, compassion, or empathy. It isn't until we actually meet these people face-to-face that we grant them true compassion and human respect. Many relationships that begin in the digital realm are self-serving and easily disposable. We use online relationships (platonic or romantic) to project ourselves and be seen in a way we wish we could be seen in real life. It may be *real* friendship for one person, but for the other it's often just an escape or a way to pass the time between real-life boyfriends or girlfriends, so when life gets better and we no longer need the distraction, the person on the other end loses what they may have considered a real friend. In a virtual world, friends are easier to manage because they are only avatars on a screen.

• • •

We may have three thousand friends on Facebook, ten thousand followers on Twitter, thousands of followers on Tumblr, and one hundred fifty "likes" for every photo we post on Instagram, but it doesn't mean we're connecting to other people in a meaningful way. In a *New York Times* article by Jenna Wortham, a number of people described the social emptiness that can result from letting our online connections stand in for face-to-face ones. One young woman said, "I wasn't calling my friends anymore . . . I was just seeing their pictures and updates." Several told Wortham socializing on social media made them feel more alienated. And yet, it seems that many people are more interested in having variety and frequency of contact, rather than building real, in-person connections. Are we poised to become a generation of sociopaths, completely shut off from the world of human emotion?

It isn't just about being disconnected from real feelings though; Facebook and Instagram do create one true, real feeling for me: they make me lonely. Just last week, I was doing my usual fifth scroll of the day through Instagram (ya know, around eight A.M.), and I came to a photo uploaded by my friend Donna. Kelly! And Brandon! Emily was there! And Dylan! Is that Steve in the background!? They were all there! Where was I and why was I not invited!? Panic. I kept scrolling. Now an upload from Steve. A group shot. They were having so much fun and I had missed the best night ever. But why had I missed it? Why hadn't I been invited? Did they all hate me? I was convinced that they did. I kept scrolling. It was quickly becoming masochistic. Next was an upload from Kelly. This was the worst one: a video. So much shouting, so much laughter. I kept thinking about how many other nights I had missed out on. I felt so lonely.

Here's an even more excruciating example: About four years ago, I introduced my four best friends to one another. I basked in the fact that I had connected them and that they got along splendidly. I was dating Samantha at the time and it also turned out that our respective friends got along. And so we had a happy group of twelve or so, attached at the hip and always hanging out. Years later, and in a less-than-graceful fashion, Samantha and I broke up and the group split down the middle. We maintained our respective friend groups, except for one or two who defected from the groups

and switched sides (traitors!). While my most loyal friends
never became close with my ex, they did stay friends with
my ex's friends and the defectors as well. Every so often
when a birthday or a celebration for one of the other group's
members comes along, I am faced with the dreaded Instagram of everyone I introduced years ago and the two groups
that split down the middle all hanging out without me. You
see, according to the universal laws of bad breakups, I can't
be invited—especially because my new significant other
would certainly come with me. But my friends are fair game.
And so I woke up the other morning to a photo posted on
Instagram, uploaded by one of the defectors, of my four
best friends who were at a party. Not just any party. My
ex's birthday party. I'm sure there were fifty more people
who attended but of course this photo contained the only
people who would make me anxious and depressed. I spi-
raled into the kind of Internet anxiety and depression that
can make you positive that you suddenly have no friends
or that you've moved down the virtual totem pole of your
social life. After maniacally texting my best friends and
asking about the night, I realized that the photo was just a
simple snapshot of a two-hour night, that no one was any
closer or less close than before, that everyone was home by
eleven thirty P.M.

Just as our real friends can make us feel as though they
are fake friends on social media, as I felt that morning seeing the "defector's" Instagram, our "friends" on social
media can often mask themselves as real friends, diluting
the actual connections we have with our real-life friends

whom we talk to on the phone or go out to dinner with. My friends aren't close with my ex, but because of social media, I convinced myself that they were. As Bill Keller wrote in a *New York Times* op-ed, "the faux friendships of Facebook and the ephemeral connectedness of Twitter [are] displacing real rapport, real intimacy." Perhaps all the chatter we slog through on a daily basis is just "virtual clutter" that is not truly connecting us. So many of us rely on social media, Facebook, smartphones, and technology for the bulk of our communication—but despite all this "connection" (or maybe *because* of it), we're not only experiencing less substantial relationships, we're also feeling more depression and loneliness.

Mark Vernon, author of *The Meaning of Friendship*, believes that our generation is lonelier because of our use of social media. We get used to what he calls the "tyranny of quantity," in which we send and receive scores of short messages but rarely have a *truly* connected conversation. We are establishing or maintaining friendships through brief, trite conversations instead of face-to-face interaction. In an aptly titled *Atlantic* article, "Is Facebook Making Us Lonely?," Stephen Marche looked deeper at the issue and mentioned a study in which 20 percent of Americans cited loneliness as the main reason they are unhappy in their lives. Across the Western world, doctors and nurses refer to an "epidemic of loneliness that is plaguing their patients." In 2010, the UK-based Mental Health Foundation released a report entitled "The Lonely Society?," which found that loneliness caused more than half of those surveyed to feel depressed.

Interestingly, many *knew* why they felt this way: Almost a third explained that they spend too much time online, rather than connecting in person. Psychologists and researchers have termed this ailment "Facebook depression." In a medical study printed in *Pediatrics*, doctors found that in addition to the "classic" Internet dangers of cyberbullying, online harassment, and sexting, one of the primary risks for adolescents is Facebook depression, which develops when teens spend too much time online in the intense virtual world of social media. How can you possibly feel loved by your friends when you are inundated with their most intensely exciting experiences all day long via social media and they are all happening without you? For teenagers in high school who are already dealing with cliques and mean girls and what lunch table to sit at *(you can't sit here)*, watching their friends leave them out every day and watching pairs of them enjoy newly founded inside jokes, this can lead to the kind of depression that the UK Mental Health Foundation talked about. As if disconnected, depressed, and lonely weren't enough, just as I felt when I scrolled through my Instagram feed to find the whole gang hanging out without me, many of us are also feeling left out. With a constant stream of friends, acquaintances, and long-lost loved ones on Facebook and Twitter raving about the amazing things they are doing and seeing, we can't help but feel more competitive and insecure about our own lives. As Daniel Gulati wrote in the *Harvard Business Review*, "[Facebook is] creating a den of comparison . . . [causing] us to recalibrate our accomplishments and reset the bar for how we define success." And the thing is, when we're sitting alone in front of a screen, it seems as though *everyone else* is in the crowd except us—even though we are *all* sitting alone in front of our screens. When I see posts of my friends hanging out without me, I try to remember that the photo is less a snapshot of the actual night and more a representation of how much fun people want to show the world (or often their ex) they are having. We try so hard to connect, to feel like a part of the virtual inner circle or cool crowd, which is of course a construction. It's all about presentation. What looks like a good time online is usually just a bunch of people at the bar staring into their phones.

So, yeah, going on Facebook or Twitter can make me feel more isolated rather than connected, and certainly more than a little insecure about my own circumstances. Some people's updates make it seem as though they have a better dinner or weekend or relationship or apartment or life. When I was single, relationships flaunted through photo albums (you know the ones) made me feel at turns nauseated, embarrassed, or tremendously alone. What's worse is that when I finally found myself in a relationship, I was the flaunter. I couldn't help it. The urge to push our relationships into other people's faces through their smartphones and computers is irresistible, and every time we do it, we reinforce the tradition. I have absolutely been *that girl* who has made daily trips to troll my ex's Facebook page, which has only served to make me feel *more* melancholy. And some people's desperate, lavish attempts to represent life in the best possible light made me want to stop spending time with them in person. (We *get* it. Your boyfriend took you to his family's Grecian island. We *get it*!) We can feel lonely when we see people uploading pictures from an event we weren't involved in, or when we read the conversations people have in the comment sections of posts and find out that we're not a part of an inside joke. And we can feel lonely when we realize that we don't truly know most of the people in our feed, have not seen many of these people *in person* in months, and have not spoken to the people we thought we were really close with on the phone because they don't talk on the phone anymore. Or we haven't made the effort to see each other because neither of us wonders what the other is up to since we see each other online, through our screens, every day. We believe we are being social with all our on-line digital interactions, but we are more isolated.

Even if my mother spent half of her day on Facebook—which she has never done, but for the sake of conversation, if she did—she'd be more likely to converse with the friends with whom she has built longtime relationships. For her, Facebook is kind of a spy tool—she uses it to see what her friends and family are posting, but in order to *truly* connect, she does what she has always done: she picks up the phone or meets someone in person.

Whenever I complain to my friends that I wasted an hour mindlessly scrolling through pet photo albums and posts about people's latest meals, I always hear the same types of scowling comments, like "I fucking hate Facebook" and "I am totally quitting Facebook, it's ruining my life." One friend has deactivated and reinstated her profile more than six times in the past three years. I have done so twice. But almost all of us come back, because either we feel left out, as though we're missing that part of our "social" lives and want to find out how some people are doing; we miss seeing photographs from parties (nobody e-mails albums through Kodak Gallery or Shutterfly anymore because we must now share our pictures with *everyone*); we saw other people scrolling through their Facebook feeds and missed the feeling of knowing what everyone else was up to; or we wanted to use Facebook to meet someone through our friends. Facebook does allow us to communicate and stay in touch without much effort, so we miss it and forget what bothered us as soon as we're out. It's kind of like an abusive relationship you keep coming back to: you forget the bad and monumentalize the good, and no sooner than you've walked away, you feel yourself looking over your shoulder and wondering if maybe you give it just one more shot things could be different . . . things could be better.

Some of my friends (and this is happening more and more frequently) who've made the final break and haven't gone back to Facebook have expressed a relief akin to getting released from prison; suddenly they don't feel so bad that they're not in love/engaged/getting married/having a child/going to Thailand on vacation, and they rediscover the gift of free time.

Free time . . . I remember it as if it were a dream; I used to stay home alone and not really think about what others were up to. Now I can see what they are doing (or liking), on Facebook, Tumblr, Twitter, Pinterest, and Instagram, through texts and e-mails—all of which can make me feel left out, depending on my mood. And I keep searching for connection—so I stay online, longer and longer, down the rabbit hole, emptily clicking through albums of quasi-friends' vacations I don't give a shit about.

Virginia Woolf wrote in *Mrs. Dalloway*, "We are not merely social beings. We are each also separate, each solitary, each alone in our own room, each miraculously our unique selves and mysteriously enclosed in that selfhood." We are *meant* to be introspective creatures and yet we hardly spend any time really considering our lives, passions, or relationships.

So many miracles. And they're all waiting for us the moment we stop gazing at our phones.

4

We're "Friends"

My mother joined Facebook in 2010. At first I panicked. Several of my friends had felt stalked by their mothers—enough to block them from their profiles—and I feared my mom would monitor my every move and that it would affect our real-life relationship. I also feared my mom would do some walking down memory lane and react, um, negatively to some of the posts or pictures already on my wall. (No, Mom, I don't smoke, and yes, that is my only tattoo.) Who even knows what kinds of horrible embarrassing posts and unflattering, late-night pictures from two years ago (a bygone era) are there waiting to be discovered by a bored lurker with too much time on her hands to click into the dregs of my Facebook profile? Or—in my paranoid fantasies—waiting to be unearthed by my mother. Thankfully, my mother hasn't been much of a stalker. She joined Facebook because all of her friends had and she was feeling left out when they talked about their status updates and tagging each other in pictures. But a few weeks after she signed up, she fell victim to one of those diet scam messages, which spammed all forty-five of her friends with the message "Wow, my legs look AMAZING! I can already feel the difference! Check out my new diet!" along with the embedded virus link. Most of her friends clicked on it (my mom is in really good shape). She was mortified, but she liked Facebook too much to disable her account. So she asked me to help her with the "ins and outs" of the social network, and of course, I obliged.

When we signed in to her account, I noticed ten or fifteen pending friend requests from people I knew she had met or recently spent time with. I started confirming the requests, when she stopped me abruptly. "What are you doing?! Stop!" she said. This confused me. I hardly ever accepted someone out of the blue but generally confirmed a friendship if a person and I had mutual friends or if we were part of the same network. My mother, however, was more discerning. As we went through her other friend requests, she routinely said, "I barely ever speak to her. Why would I accept her as one of my friends?" Or, "I haven't seen him in months! I wouldn't consider him a good friend." Finally, there was, "Eh, I had dinner with her last week and it was boring. Don't accept." My mother and I gauged "friendship" in massively different ways.

Her comments stuck with me the next time I signed in to my own Facebook account. At the time, I had 1,462 friends. Yes—1,462. If someone had asked me how many *real* friends I had, I would probably have told them I had fifteen good friends (except when I'm scrolling through Instagram and I suddenly feel positive that I have none) and about forty acquaintances with whom I was friendly. When I stopped to think about it, 1,462 friends seemed kind of embarrassing, so I spent what ended up being four hours of a Saturday afternoon going through every name in my friend list, trying to decipher how many of them I *truly* considered friends. My guidelines were simple: If I could picture their face when reading their name, I would count them as an acquaintance. If I had spoken to them (on IM, Gchat, via e-mail or text, or actually *live* on the telephone) in the recent past (i.e., within three weeks), I would consider them a friend. As I went through the list of names, I found that out of my 1,462 "friends," I could not recall who 478 of these people actually were—not even by looking at their profile photos—or why I had accepted their "friendship" in the first place. Of the 984 individuals that I could at least say I "knew," I had spoken to only 140 of them in the recent past. From that group, twenty-one were coworkers, one was my live-in girlfriend, another was my roommate, one was my mom, and one was my dog (whom I had made a profile for and then friended myself . . .)—all of whom, for the most part, I was expected to talk to every day.

This information astounded me. I had let 478 people—*whom I did not know at all*—see my photos, read my status updates, and know my whereabouts. When I vaguely considered my Facebook friends, I thought of Amy and Brenda and Dylan and Steve. But the reality was there was this faceless horde that I had allowed into my innermost thoughts and private moments. Was it creepy? It was slightly creepy. Facebook gave me the cozy illusion of security and closeness. But the notion that only my inner circle is privy to my information is horrifyingly misleading.

That word: *friend*. To me, it's always meant someone you might confide in, someone you want to share things with, so when I shared photos and updates with my friends on my Facebook wall, it was always with the implicit understanding—or the unwarranted assumption—that the people I was sharing with were actually *friends*. When I got engaged, I got Facebook messages from around the world congratulating me. Sure, it was great to have the support and to know others were excited as well, but who *were* these people? I didn't know any of their faces and could not pronounce most of their names. Two messages in particular stood out: "Kim it is Katia from Russia. You look happy happy. You lucky girl to find a man like that. I follow you forever and now follow husband too! Love from Moscow!" My fiancée (the one named Lexi with the long brown hair wearing a bikini in the most recent upload) was not pleased. The other message that stood out was a bit more disturbing. "You dumb lesbian. Marriage is between a man and a woman. Tell me where you live and I'll show you a real man." Oh, okay. Cool. So nice to get this message from one of my "friends" on Facebook. I quickly unfriended him. But why was I friends with him in the first place? And why had I ever called these strangers "friends" if even for social media purposes?

What does friendship even mean in the context of all this easy clicking? We become "friends" with people who may have been on the fringe of the groups we hung out with in college, high school, or even grade school; random people we have fun with at parties; friends of friends we see once a year; or others we've met through work or our shared networks. Although they may "like" some of our photos or status updates, we don't actually speak to many of these random acquaintances, who are often closer to "stranger" on the friend-stranger scale. And yet they know personal information about us (or are a click away from it) because we share it willingly.

For many, the definition of friendship has expanded to include someone they are connected to online regardless of whether they see or talk regularly to that person or even particularly trust them. In some cases, we've never even met our friends. But we still tend to have blind faith in those we've brought into our circle. We become "friends" online at a much faster rate than we do in person, which is completely ironic, given that most people I spoke with claim to believe that face-to-face interaction is necessary for a *true* trusting friendship. When I was growing up, all kids were instructed never to talk to strangers. Now we're running out and *looking* for strangers to talk to—sometimes if only to get our "numbers up." The more "friends" you have, the more popular you are, the higher your self-worth . . . right? Right??

It's funny how quick we are to welcome people into our circle, especially when so many of us are more likely to lie in our online profiles or conversations that take place on the Internet, compared to when we talk to someone in person. When I polled my "friends" (so mainly a few friends and mostly strangers), more than a third admitted to lying online, whether it was about a topic as mundane as a favorite movie (to sound more interesting) or something more serious, like their job or relationship status. David Holmes, a psychologist at Manchester Metropolitan University, examined how honest we are on our social networking profiles and found that up to *40 percent* of the information posted could be falsified. This isn't surprising, as most social media sites provide their users with the ability to be whoever they want for whatever kind of attention they crave and don't ask us to verify any of it. And we don't ask our online friends to prove what they say is true, because we probably won't be seeing them in person anytime soon.

And yet we rarely think about those to whom we're linked or what that means. I don't offer a ton of personal information on Facebook or any social media for that matter, but photos and friends' tagged items add up, and depending on privacy settings, friends of friends can sometimes see posts, so we all end up revealing more than we think we do, to people we do not know at all. I had an old friend—we'll call her Allison—who took a turn down crazy street when we were about twenty-five. She had always been a little "clingy," but her seemingly mild psychotic tendencies flared up at some point and I needed to take a few months (years) away from the friendship. (Think: *Single White Female*. Remember the episode of

Beverly Hills, 90210 where Kelly starts hanging out with Tara, whom she met during a stint in rehab? And then Tara tries to become her? And finds the same jean jacket that Kelly has? And then tries to force Kelly into a double suicide? It was actually nothing like that but I love that episode and my friend had definitely become creepy in an *SWF* type of way.) I stopped calling her for a while. She would call and call, and I would text back that I was really busy for a couple of weeks, or whatever excuse I could make. Then things got a bit creepier. I would be at a bar and she would show up. (I had checked in on Foursquare.) She would randomly pass me when I was walking out to lunch from work. (I worked in Times Square at the time at MTV, and I think we all know that no one hangs out there unless they are a tourist or an employee who works in the area. She was neither.) I recognized that she was obsessively following me on Facebook, Twitter, and Foursquare and was pretending to "randomly end up" at the places I was; she was simply following (and mirroring) my every move. I had no choice but to unfriend and block her. I felt terrible about it but she truly left me no choice. I didn't want to end up at an overlook spot tied up inside my car like Kelly! I made one mistake though. My privacy settings were still set so that "friends of friends" could see my profile and almost all of the information on it. While she was blocked from Twitter and Foursquare, her Facebook stalking raged via our mutual friends' pages. The stalking continued, but she knew I'd blocked her so now she was mad. Luckily, a few weeks later she moved to California to see (stalk) an old boyfriend. My saga was over, but I certainly learned my lesson the hard way about what I am sharing and with whom I am sharing it when I click "Post," "Update," or "Check In." There is no such thing as privacy online.

I still count only five or six people as my closest, most dear, *best* friends and do not define them as such because of how frequently I speak to them or how many photos of them are posted on my Facebook wall. I know they are my friends because I call them when I'm upset; I can trust them and be sure that they'll keep my secrets; if they were in trouble, I would drop everything to find them and help them. Trust is the operative word and that quality truly separates my real friends and the "friends" I have online.

Every once in a while, one of my Facebook "friends" will try to start a chat with me. My real-life friends get in touch with me over text or e-mail, or they may even call if they're feeling really ambitious, so I'm not sure why I keep my Facebook chat on. Maybe for curiosity's sake. The people who contact me on Facebook chat fall into two categories. They are either *Top Model* fans I accepted right after the show was aired or my mom's friends (you know the kind, the ones who are *always* on Facebook posting chain letters and long sob stories and stalking their daughters). As for the MTV and *Top Model* fans who contact me through Facebook, the thing is—and perhaps there is no way of saying the following without sounding obnoxious, so please bear with me—I was constantly amazed by the illusion (or delusion) of connectedness that these (almost) strangers felt toward me. They believed that the mere acceptance of a friend request was the first step in our budding friendship—and I suppose that is exactly what I encouraged when I accepted them. By clicking "confirm" I basically said, "Yes, we are friends, go for it, contact me. Do what *friends* do." I acknowledge I was complicit in making them feel they could write me notes like "Hey top model!!! Your dinner looked great last night. Will you cook for me sometime? Ps you were my favorite. I was rooting for u!"

In his book *Virtually You*, Dr. Elias Aboujaoude discusses the danger of losing our sense of privacy. "With so much of our facts readily available online for anyone to consult," he says, "control over our personal business has become a chimerical goal. This can threaten our self-possession . . . The small zone of privacy that we all need and that is crucial to our psychological equilibrium is nowhere to be found." Without a second thought, I had blindly and willingly accepted so many people into my virtual circle of friends that people I didn't know existed ended up knowing all this stuff about me. I had been careless with my privacy. Uh-oh. I had welcomed strangers into my dinners, friendships, and even birthday parties! I remember being inundated with Facebook messages on my last birthday. People whose Facebook profiles stated they currently lived in Oman or Bangladesh or the Netherlands were asking me the address of my birthday party (they wanted to stop by, of course!) and others were sending me strange little emoticons of cakes and candles on my profile. Over the last couple of years, the cake emoticons started appearing on my page when I uploaded a photo of my mom or dad on their birthdays. (One stranger wrote, "Happy birthday to your parents Kimmy! I'd love to meet them one day!" What? *What?*)

One study completed at Western Illinois University demonstrated that the number of friends we have indicates how narcissistic we are, that our "drive for attention" is behind our need to seek a wider and wider audience. Some people friend more people just to feel as though they are part of a larger circle. Maybe they didn't get enough love and attention in their formative years.

The fact is it's impossible to sustain hundreds of friend-ships. British evolutionary anthropologist Robin Dunbar, who studies friendships formed through the Internet, ar-gues that humans cannot process more than 150 friendships at any given point in their lives. He actually says our brains may not be big enough to handle them. Once we surpass this number—which is called Dunbar's Number—some people start falling by the wayside. Perhaps human beings are simply not wired to exist in the Facebook construct.

Our Facebook news feeds can't tell the difference be-tween our actual friends and those we have randomly confirmed—or felt obligated to confirm. Posts from faux friends clog our feed, while those from the most significant people in our real lives are shuffled along with the rest, flat-tening the friendship landscape until strangers and stead-fast pals are given democratic treatment. Everyone's just a JPEG to be clicked and expanded on or shrunk, confirmed or ignored. Of course, in recent years, Facebook has added the option of hiding people from news feeds so that we can stop seeing posts from the people we truly don't want to know about (or for me, people who post too many kitten photos, even if they are my best friends in real life). The issue with this new function, however, is that when you're already friends with seven hundred too many people on Facebook, it's nearly impossible to go through and hide all the right feeds. Plus, as social media addicts, we are also secretly worried that if we hide too much, we will *miss* something. The whole thing is so exhausting. Which brings us back to the point that we probably shouldn't be accepting people as "friends" if we don't want to know anything about them!

A few years ago, I missed a close friend's birthday party because she sent the invite on Facebook. It had arrived with sixteen other invitations—to comedy shows with terrible titles (one was called *Doogie and Doggie*—why must people do these things?), birthday spectaculars for people I'd never heard of, invitations to like people's new books or plays or films or new jobs (I don't understand inviting someone to "like" a new job), a gallery opening for unappetizing drawings of people eating—and assuming they were all from people I didn't know, I insta-deleted all of them.

I also missed my friend's postings about the party because my feed was saturated with random strangers' enlightening status updates, like "At Bloomingdales :) Happy . . . I love spending money that's not mine :) thanx mom" (*Who was this person?*); relationship notifications from the oversexed and overinvolved; and general complaints and comments, like "classic L.A. problem: drive to dinner and then direct to the bar? Or drive to dinner, drive home, drop off the car and cab it to the bar?" (*We get it. You're going out tonight. Good for you.*) My Facebook feed is cluttered with too much information that is not improving my life in any way. The mundane and/or blatantly self-promotional posts make me angry—especially when I miss notices that would have been valuable to my *real* life. These posts are boring and useless time-sucks that are preventing me from really connecting with the people I actually know and want to stay connected with. The other day, a friend of mine wrote me an angry text about not congratulating her on a new job she'd posted about on Facebook. I hadn't seen it, but this is the problem: even though we are all inundated with constant information from hundreds of people, we also hold each other up to the expectation that our friends will all see and react to everything we post. And the worst part is that all the promotional and fluff posts make me angry at myself too, because I could think of countless posts and uploads of my own advertising my restaurant, or an article I was in, or even this book. It makes me embarrassed of myself, though I know the feeling won't stop me from posting and self-promoting in the future.

As our online social circles expand, I am often baffled by what some of my online friends share; their status updates make me wonder how they could be so open to people they don't really know—and whether they believe they really know every person in their friend list. A few months ago, one of my friends' grandfather died. Before she even had a chance to tell her friends about it over text or on the phone, she had posted the news on Facebook, Twitter, and Four-square. (Though at least she didn't check into her grand-father's funeral—I was not planning on admitting this, but I definitely checked into the funeral home. Sigh.) She also updated her status on Facebook with something like "RIP, Grandpa. We'll miss you!" I was really surprised that she posted such delicate news in such an informal manner to her twelve hundred friends—at least 20 percent of whom she most likely didn't know or rarely spoke to. I wasn't sure if I should comment on such a serious, sad post. (I think I'd be appalled if I died and someone just commented on the status update. They might as well just "like" it.) The news of her grandfather's death became just a blip on the screen. In a way, it lessened the significance of his passing, and I wondered how many people registered it compassionately with the seriousness it deserved.

That I found out about her grandfather's death through my Facebook feed also clarified that we were no longer that close. Other friends have commented that they know they are no longer "really friends" with people when they learn about an engagement or pregnancy—or any significant life event—from Facebook or social media. Today, e-mails and texts are considered more intimate. Dr. Wicker explains that "relationships are built upon layers of trust. Blasting out personal information does not build trust or increase intimacy. It just blasts out information."

Maybe it's wrong and insensitive of me to judge my friend in her time of grief. After all, each person reacts in her own way and has the right to share news however she pleases—and yct I couldn't help but think that my friend's hashtagged cries for help were more about getting the attention of as many people as possible at one time, sort of like texting a mass booty call (yes, I just compared her grandfather's death to a booty call). Each of her posts reminded me of the teary overshares reality stars spit out whenever they are desperate for more screen time. I couldn't figure out whether she was feeling actual sadness or grief. Maybe she just needed and wanted the attention and didn't care if the people reading her post were friends or not as long it was read. But then I realized that I wasn't so different from her. None of us with twelve hundred friends on Facebook are. When my cycle of *America's Next Top Model* was airing, I accepted almost every Facebook friend request that came my way. I wanted the exposure because that is what my life was about then. And when I blogged for the *Huffington Post* or did segments on *MTV News*, I was happy that I could blast out and publicize my work. My restaurant shared its events on Facebook and I am happy to post them myself as well. I may not be trying to get "attention" in the same way that my friend was with her grandpa death tweets, but I certainly am trying to get business and exposure. I'm sure many of you who are reading this have already seen Facebook messages and events, tweets, Instagrams, and Tumblrs from me trying to get you to buy this book (thank you, BTW). The problem, however, is that when we do strive to heighten our attention or exposure via Facebook, we tend to end up with hundreds of friends we don't truly consider "friends" and our privacy and "real" friendships are at risk of being compromised. Once again, I'm embarrassed by my need to self-promote online but not enough that I can or will stop myself: it's too easy and I'm afraid I will miss out on an opportunity if I put on the brakes.

The wonderful and creepy thing about social media is that somebody is always out there (new friends and loved ones, new customers who will buy our crap) even if we don't know who those somebodies are. We've entered a new realm, where people feel comfortable sharing *a lot*. We all have our own rules and inner monologues about what's acceptable and what's too much. Some are like me—hovering in the bubble of willful delusion that we know every one of our virtual friends. Others are like my friend who told everyone about her grandfather's funeral because she wanted to feel the mass-level love. There are precious few like my ultra-discerning mom, whose "friends" are all really friends. But whatever strictures you apply to yourself, once you go on-line, you're part of the oversharing club to some degree.

My friend Brenda told me a story about her friend Donna that mocked the attention-grabbing overshare club we've all joined. Donna was at an Apple Store, browsing through Facebook on one of their public computers. About thirty minutes after she left, she received a notification on her phone that her cousin and eleven other people had commented on her status. She also had nine missed calls on her phone. Texts are one thing but missed calls mean business. Donna thought to herself, *Nobody calls me anymore unless there's something imminently important to discuss.* Donna signed on to Facebook on her phone in order to see what the comments referred to, because she hadn't updated her status in a few days. (I'm still not sure why Donna had even signed in to Facebook at the store when she could access it on her smartphone, but this is what we do.) Next to her name, the following status update stared back at her: "HIV test came back positive. Bummer." In the twenty or so minutes that Donna had left her Facebook account open at the Apple Store, somebody played a practical joke on her by posting to each of her 822 friends that she was HIV-positive—and that she was ridiculous enough to tell everyone she knew via Facebook. I thought the most amusing (disturbing) part was that Donna's cousin actually commented on this status and wrote, "OMG I'm so sorry! Let me know if there is anything I can do!" Apparently even an AIDS-related announcement didn't merit a phone call. (Also, imagine "OMG" as a reaction?! Amazing.)

For many people there is *nothing strange at all* about posting such incredibly personal information on a website that immediately disseminates it to hundreds—or millions, depending on your privacy settings. When I first got Facebook in 2004, I was very cautious about what I posted. Wesleyan University, where I went to college, was one of the first schools to get Facebook. It was "the Facebook" then and it was reserved only for college kids. My first memories of Facebook involve being in Olin Library at Wesleyan. I had a crush on a girl named Emily and Emily loved the Facebook, so I decided I better become a pro at this new and exciting website. Our relationship started because I sent her a Facebook message. I watched her, across

Olin, log on to one of the computers about two hundred feet from me, read my message, and type a few words, and before I knew it, I had a friend request from her. The rest was history (until we broke up two years later). "The Facebook" was mainly for all of us to stalk our campus crushes and ascertain whether or not they were single. I think that is how almost all of us used it. No one was sending invitations or "liking" things. We wanted to know if we could date each other. And of course we liked looking at profile photos, but people weren't really posting photos otherwise (there was no such thing as the mobile upload, so almost everything was done by computer). Gradually, though, the Facebook became Facebook, the world of users got exponentially larger, I got used to sharing information with my growing friend base, and then I started posting what I would have previously told only my closest friends. The attention I got from sharing my thoughts and the details of my life was exhilarating. I loved seeing people's responses and feeling so connected to so many that I got addicted to updating my status and posting even more photos and links, just so more and more people would comment. It didn't take long for me to stop thinking about the potential consequences— the fact that many people had access to the details of my private life or the fact that the ephemeral details of my life (some of which would embarrass my future self) would live forever online. Years later, a different girlfriend was perusing my account and found that very first Facebook message to Emily. She didn't like its flirtatious tone even though it was four years later. We got into a fight. Perfect.

This incessant documentation leads to a weird sense that the feelings that you felt four years ago for a person still exist in some dimension. The fact that life online has its own properties, its own immortality, its own weight or weightlessness . . . this can be comforting if our lives at home or with our families are not going the way we want them to and we want to distract ourselves from our real life—or our difficult off-line relationships—with whatever community we have established online. We can receive the stimulation and attention online that is lacking in our off-line lives. Some people even begin to create double lives and grow more distant from their real, everyday existences, and many have replaced the most important real-life, human-to-human interactions with online relationships. My clingy-turned-psychotic friend Tara? I was looking her up on Facebook recently (I like to confirm for myself every once in a while that she still lives in California) and I saw that she was posting photos of herself from a red carpet and tagging various celebrities. I thought to myself, *How could Tara have edged herself into that scene?* She'd never had a job as far as I knew and was the farthest thing from charismatic. Yet night after night, I watched her post glamorous photos (never with anyone, just of her) and write things like "My life is amazing right now! So blessed." Confused but somewhat bored with my conundrum, I moved on. Maybe she'd changed? Two weeks later, I found out she had moved away from California and back in with her parents in New Jersey. It turns out it really isn't hard to find a "step-and-repeat" or red carpet and pretend it's somewhere else with someone else. All it takes is @-ing someone and everyone just assumes you're with them. It was a nice campaign she led for a while, but (at least in my mind) it ended abruptly and embarrassingly. Her double life was surely about pretending to others that she was leading a lavish, successful, and exciting life. But I think it was mostly about escaping from her own life and problems and living in a fantasy world. What better place to do so than social media, where you may be living a fantasy but the comments and reactions are "real."

Over time, given the easy escape that our online accounts allow, we may begin to subconsciously choose to be distracted by them rather than working on the issues complicating our real lives. In this way, the delusion of an online connection hinders genuine off-line bonds.

While on vacation in Florida, I spent some time at the bar of my dad's golf club working on this book and consuming Bloody Marys. Steve, one of the golf pros, asked me what I was writing. When I told him what it was about, an anxious excitement came over his face. "Facebook ended my marriage," he said, most likely expecting me to react with surprise or shock. Of course, he didn't know that he was the fortieth person who had told me the exact same thing—or that he was talking to the Queen of Social Media–Related Breakups (well, at least in New York City's lesbian community).

Steve told me that his wife, Cindy, had opened a Facebook account about a year before they got married. At first, he was concerned by how much she was using it, but his concerns weren't serious enough for him to question their relationship. As time went on, however, her addiction became deeper. She would come home from work, go straight to the couch or desk without saying hello to him, and sign in to Facebook, where she would remain for the next five or six hours before going to bed. A year into their marriage, it was so bad that Steve felt like he was living with a Facebook zombie. He often found himself eating dinner alone and spent weekends out of the house while Cindy stayed inside, trolling the site. He was also doing all the household chores—making dinner, cleaning, and doing laundry. Finally, after couple's therapy and numerous attempts at trying to get her to decrease her usage, Steve gave Cindy an ultimatum: it was Facebook or their marriage. She told him that of course she chose their marriage and deleted her Facebook account immediately. Two weeks later, he found her hiding in the garage, signed in to a new account that she had created using a different name. He filed for divorce the next day.

If Robin Dunbar is correct and we may only be able to handle 150 friendships, perhaps the more online friendships we cut out, the happier we'll be. We'll feel more in control of our lives and less deluded about the quality of our friendships. We will actually *know* the people we're friends with and be able to manage these relationships.

So why can't we just delete the people that we don't want to hear from, the people we *don't* want to be our friends? For some, the action of unfriending someone is an even bigger affront than not calling a person back or rejecting them as a friend in real life. (Many people avoid doing the latter and just let friendships fade away, whereas clicking "unfriend" is an act of complete and outright rejection.) There are countless people whom I would love to unfriend on Facebook. There are a lot of friends I met during tennis camp, for instance, who truly have turned into some very strange people. I don't want to see their feeds or wonder about when they chose to start a Wallflowers cover band. (Imagine a Wallflowers cover band? Of all things . . .) And then there are the scores of my mom's friends whom I love but truly don't need polluting my feed with posts that almost always start with "Before you read this, wish on a star" and always end with "Now send this to seven friends and you will get your wish!" Horrific. But the fact is, I still care about these people and wouldn't want to hurt their feelings. I know that if they noticed that I was no longer their "friend," they would wonder how I could do something so insulting and then I might get a call from my mom asking why I unfriended her friend, and that is exactly the kind of conversation I hope to avoid. Sometimes I hide their feeds, but there are so many people who fit the above descriptions it feels like an endless task. Apparently, not inviting these same people to parties, forgetting to call them back from time to time, and essentially having no friendship with them are less of an affront than merely removing them from my virtual friend circle. Etiquette guru Emily Post would approve of the decision to unfriend. On her website she advises, "You may find a time when it is necessary to [un]friend—your list is too big, you've had a falling-out/break-up, or someone has been harassing or bothering you. It is definitely okay to unfriend someone you no longer feel comfortable being connected with." I agree with Emily. In fact, I think we should have an annual celebration of unfriending the people whose activities we wish we were no longer privy to on social media even though we haven't been able to muster up the courage to finally click "Unfriend." In August 2013, there was a National Unfriending Day. What a great idea. Perhaps next year, we'll start a National Unfriending My Ex Day. It may be just what we (I) need.

My wife and I were cooking dinner with my parents one night last summer and my mom (who is literally the nicest person of all time and the last person I'd ever imagine unfriending someone) asked awkwardly, "Kimmy, would you mind showing me later how to stop being friends with someone on Facebook?" (See? She didn't even know it was called "unfriend." Bravo, Mom!) So I could have gone two ways with this. I could have simply told her, or I could dig a little deeper to find out who she wanted to unfriend. (I love parent gossip!) But before I could make my decision, my wife exclaimed, "Carol! Who do you want to unfriend?! Do tell, do tell!" My mom shifted a little bit. "Well . . . umm . . ." We carried on, asking her who. "Okay, fine," she said, "I want to defriend Samantha." (Samantha was my ex-girlfriend who had unfriended me, most of my friends, and my dog but somehow had decided to stay "friends" with my mom [!].) It was a brilliant moment. My mom unfriend-ing my ex. Does it truly get any better than that?

I used to think it was silly that my mother refuses to accept people on Facebook if she doesn't feel close enough with them or doesn't want to be privy to their daily status updates. But maybe she's got the right idea; her feed isn't overloaded, and more importantly, she knows who her friends are. So at the risk of pissing off a large number of people in my fourth-to-seventh-degree levels of acquaintance, I finally decided to follow my mom's lead and delete the 478 people on my friend list I didn't know. That left me with 984 "friends"—834 more people than I'm able to keep track of, according to Dr. Dunbar. It's a start.

5

It doesn't take much more than a perusal of the comments section of an online article or a YouTube video to know that the net is a powder keg of emotional turmoil and destruction—one little word or sentence or gesture can set off a major war.

The Internet stokes the darkest parts of our personalities: abusive attacks over e-mail, unfiltered texts and tweets, passive-aggressive photo commentary, and one-liner status-update one-upmanship. The daggers can be passive, conveyed by a *lack* of response. Or, our newly acquired ADD speeds up the way we react online and removes most of whatever filter we may have, rendering us incapable of thinking through what we want to say—and making us more willing and able to be cruel to each other. And with the screen to shield us (no matter how many cracks you have in it), we don't even have to deal with the consequences.

I have often endured the electronic dagger, so much so in relationships that I once attempted to establish a cardinal relationship rule: two people who are dating cannot, under any circumstances, activate the "read receipt" feature on their iPhones or be connected on BlackBerry Messenger (BBM). Now, you may recall my story of how the "read receipt" functionality played a significant role in certain fights I've had with my wife. I am saying that I think this is a cardinal relationship rule. I didn't say that I had any luck following it.

I first learned of the power of the "read receipt" during a certain summer, when I was involved with a girl named Brenda and still had a BlackBerry. She was as beautiful as she was paranoid, and as witty and hilarious as she was suspicious and scheming. And at the time, I was a member of the masses who failed to think twice about adding a girlfriend to my BBM. Constant contact seemed so romantic, so close. I love seeing when you're typing!

For the non–BlackBerry users out there, BBMing is similar to texting on an iPhone if "read receipt" is turned on. This is nothing like texting or e-mailing. And it's more involved than instant messenger (IM), though similarly if the phone isn't turned on or the person isn't available (on another call or texting with someone else), they won't get the message. Unlike IM, you can activate a "read receipt" indicator so that once you hit send, one of two indicators will appear next to your message: a "D" for "Delivered," which means that your recipient's phone has received the message but he or she has not yet read it; or an "R" for "Read" (with a time and date), which means your recipient has read your message. If there is nothing accompanying your message, it hasn't been delivered because the person you are trying to reach is either on the phone or their phone is off or out of cell service range. When you are having a typed conversation on one of these devices, your thought process is revealed: each time you click the mini keys on a BlackBerry or iPhone, the other person's phone shows ellipses (or, in the case of old-school BBM, a notice that says, *"Kimmy Stolz is typing . . ."*), so the person on the receiving end knows exactly when you started typing, how long it is taking you to type your message, and if you stopped to think during the middle of your sentence. I hate the stop-and-think. Never leads to anything good.

Brenda and I were in constant contact on BBM. We would message each other from the moment we woke up until the moment we went to sleep, during meetings, across tables, and—rudely, I'll admit—during dinners with our friends. We sent notes about anything and everything—what we were doing, who we were with, where we were going. Sarcastic, biting, and funny messages were interspersed with "I miss you" and "Where are you?" and general information about our lives.

All these notes made us feel quite close, but the constant access became a problem. We were so tethered to each other that if one of us took more than a couple of minutes to write back, the other would go crazy. Our conversations were so frequent and intense that any break became suspicious.

One night, about a month into our relationship, while

Brenda was working late, I went out with my friends to a bar in the West Village. Like a lot of bars in the city, it was on the basement level and had little to no cell phone service. My friends and I were seated at a table in one of the enclaves that, while spotty, had enough service for my BlackBerry. We drank bottles of Malbec and Cava, and as usual, I was BBMing with Brenda, though I had put my phone on silent to save the battery. (God forbid my phone died and I was unreachable. That was basically the same as cheating!)

The first mistake I made that night was to read one of Brenda's messages and not write back right away. The dreaded "R" that appeared on her message along with my lack of response did not make her happy. While I privately enjoyed a little thrill at not being at her beck and call, she hated the idea that I was doing something more exciting than responding to her message and assumed I was flirting with someone else (which I was not). Two minutes later, I was surprised that my BlackBerry began buzzing and shaking, even though it was in silent mode. I watched as the phone moved around on the table in front of me, knowing it could only mean one thing: the PING.

The dreaded PING was originally created by BlackBerry maker Research In Motion (RIM) as a means of getting the attention of a phone's owner, perhaps in an emergency. Many, like me, leave our phones on silent to prevent unnecessary distractions. As long as the phone has service, though, the PING function will override the user's current setting and make the BlackBerry vibrate, flash, and beep, regardless of where you are or what you are doing. In an emergency, I would imagine this to be useful. In a relation-ship (or a business meeting), it is not. That night I began to realize that each time I failed to answer a BBM within four or five minutes—even if we were having a mundane conversation about nothing at all—Brenda would PING me, demanding my attention and response. It was annoy-ing and aggressive. And I totally admit that I did the same thing to her many, many nights.

The only thing in the PING! family that is even more ag-gressive and annoying is the more and more frequent abuse of the Find My iPhone application. One of the great things about having an iPhone is that if you lose it, you can sign in to iCloud or an application called Find My iPhone and locate your iPhone. The application also has a great feature for those of us who generally lose their phone while walk-ing around their own apartment. It's on the shelf! On the terrace! In the refrigerator (yep, I've done that)! If you click "Play Sound," your iPhone will make a shrill pinging noise until you find it and click a button. Whether your phone is set to silent, vibrate, or loud, this same vibrate-and-ping noise will occur. Now, if I were to guess, I'd say most people in serious relationships know each other's Apple ID (which is all you need to sign in to Find My iPhone). We are always on each other's phones, downloading music, playing Candy Crush, ordering SeamlessWeb. If my wife's phone is dead and she wants to do any of the aforementioned, she just uses mine. It's normal. But what's *not* normal is something that happened to my friend Kelly. She was out to dinner with four of her friends and happened to be in a fight with her boyfriend at the time. She was annoyed and placed her phone facedown on the table (note that it was still *on* the table) and put it on silent. She had to at least enjoy one course with us without maniacally texting. About nine minutes later, a shrill noise came from her side of the table. We all knew the noise. But why was Kelly trying to locate her phone when she and we all knew it was right in front of her? And then we realized it. It could only be one thing: Kelly's boyfriend had become frustrated with Kelly's lack of response and had subsequently signed on to Kelly's Find My iPhone or iCloud application and clicked "Play Sound." Outrageous and inappropriate as it was, it got Kelly's attention. She picked up her phone, embarrassed, and went outside to call her boyfriend. She never came back in. (That sounded really ominous. She's still alive, she just left dinner. But anyway, enough about her, back to the story about me . . .)

So around midnight, Brenda sent me a note that said she was going home to sleep. We BBMed "good night" and I went back to the conversation with my friends. Shortly thereafter, we left our table and went to dance in the back room, where there was barely any service. I put my phone in my pocket in case anyone (Brenda) needed to reach me. Around two A.M., my friends and I decided to go home, and we walked upstairs to street level. As my BlackBerry regained consciousness, my pocket was attacked by buzzing. Clicking to my BBM, I found four messages from Brenda:

"How's your night?"

"Wow. You're so shady."

[PING!]

[PING!]

[PING!]

[PING!]

"Cool. I get it."

I couldn't tell what time each of these messages had come in (they had come in pairs as my service was spotty), but I could only imagine where Brenda's mind had traveled over the previous two hours. I knew where she was coming from; I wanted replies from her as much as she wanted them from me, and I hate waiting for people to text me back.

Despite the hour, I called to check in, but she screened. I could tell she was doing this because I heard two and a half rings before her voice mail picked up. That was one good thing about being addicted to my phone: I knew ring patterns by heart. Zero or one and a quarter rings means the phone is off or out of service (in New York, this usually means someone is on the subway—or in an underground bar); four or five and a half rings before voice mail means the person missed your call (or was "missing" it on purpose); and anything in between, like the almost-three rings I got that night, means a screen—the person you're trying to reach doesn't want to deal with you at that particular moment (or they do, and they're making you work for it) and has pressed ignore your call. I hung up, confused and bothered. I thought Brenda wanted to talk to me—why else would she send me those BBMs? I left a message, pleading with her to talk to me. Then, like clockwork, a BBM came through: "I don't want to talk to you. Leave me alone." Now, anyone who has dated me knows that this kind of statement will lead to one thing and one thing only: another phone call. I called Brenda again. Once again, two and a half rings. Then came two BBMs:

"So as soon as I go to sleep, you turn off your phone so that you don't have to be reachable? Why would you not want to be reachable? I'm assuming she was very pretty."

And:

"Hope it was worth it."

• • •

In a way, Brenda and I were playing a new digital version of hard to get, and it was all about control. If I took three minutes to respond, she would take almost four. If I took twenty-five seconds to write back, she would take twenty-six. It was a game, and Brenda played it well. Exhilarating and exhausting, it went on for our entire yearlong off-and-on relationship.

I considered each of her zings (and nonresponses) to be electronic daggers and imagine that if we had spoken on the phone or if we were in person, Brenda would *not* have said the things she wrote. But that's the clever (and enraging) thing about texting and social media: one can be as nasty or passive-aggressive as humanly possible without having to endure (or even fully imagine) the reaction of the person on the other end of the exchange. In the digital realm, people can write things that they would normally be too embarrassed, afraid, or self-respecting to say. The ability to text, e-mail, or instant-message from behind a screen allows people to get their point across without having to listen to the other person's side of the story. The writer never has to accept the other person's point of view, and the unfairness or cruelty of the comment is never reflected back in their face. Plus, we can always just choose to turn off our phones when we've had enough (or if we actually start to feel something).

I have found that it's so much easier to write quick, mean notes over text or e-mail if I am frustrated, angry, or upset. Dr. Aboujaoude cites Dr. Jeanne B. Funk, a psychologist at the University of Toledo, who is concerned that we're becoming less moral and more cruel, because the "desensitization makes us bypass the moral centers of the brain and robs us of our ability to empathize." Dr. Wicker notes that it is certainly easier to be aggressive through electronic communication, as "we escape the consequences of our aggression when we do not have to endure the empathic pain that face-to-face communication would likely bring." I have had brutal fights over text but as soon as I am in the same room as the person, the fight seems to die down and things are okay again. How could I tell them such mean things in person? It just seems cruel. Over text, it's a game and anything goes. Simply put, we are more capable of feeling empathy when we are looking at someone's face, at their eyes, seeing and receiving their feelings.

According to Gary Small, MD, and Gigi Vorgan, the authors of *iBrain: Surviving the Technological Alteration of the*

Modern Mind, the "empathy deficit may not be limited to just young adult and teenage brains. Empathy is learned, but it can be un-learned as well." They found that teenagers "were much slower to recognize" a happy facial expression after playing a violent video game. They also found that the neural circuits of both "digital natives" and "digital immigrants" were affected after only *one week* of Internet activity. Technology can impact brains of any age. None of us is immune.

Dr. Aboujaoude argues that through the Internet, we turn into different people. He writes, "Gentleness, common courtesy, and the little niceties that announce us as well mannered, civilized and sociable members of the species are quickly stripped away to reveal a completely naked, often unpleasant human being." We just type out responses without filtering them properly. Because we are behind our little screens, it's a lot easier to insult each other, to type some horrible statement or write something rude or out of line. After all, we're not saying it to your face. We can't see your reaction. It does not register in our mind that what we write may hurt you. We have, in a way, forgotten that you have feelings.

Cyberbullying isn't just some middle school phenomenon—it's what we're dishing out on an increasingly regular basis. Living behind our screens enables us to be crueler than we may intend, inhabiting avatars that are more reckless, selfish, dangerous, and lacking in compassion, even toward the people we love. We rely on our screens to give us the confidence to express our feelings—however passive—or overtly aggressive. As Dr. Aboujaoude explains, "our online self is also dangerous and irresponsible, running roughshod over our caution and self-control. It can encourage us to pursue unrealistic or unhealthy goals . . . it can encourage us to behave more selfishly and recklessly." I recently gave a speech in Houston to an all-girls school on social media, sexting, and cyberbullying. I spent the morning and part of the afternoon with the student body, about nine hundred high school girls, and heard their stories and the ways that social media was affecting their lives. Like any other high school kids today, they had horror stories relating to sexting and cyberbullying, and of course thousands of anecdotes of feeling left out, lonely, or ganged up on by social media. I'd heard most of it before. But then they mentioned something called "sub-tweeting" or "subliminal tweeting." I consider myself pretty well connected but this was the first I'd heard of this new activity on Twitter. Sub-tweeting is when someone tweets a statement about another person but does not mention them by name. For instance, if Kelly, Dylan, and I are having lunch and Valerie sits down (and Kelly clearly does not want to sit with Valerie because she despises her), Kelly might tweet, "Guess someone didn't get the memo that we didn't want to sit with her." Kelly has sub-tweeted. Dylan, Valerie, and I all follow Kelly, so we will see the tweet and all secretly know that she is talking about Valerie. This anonymous tweeting gives us a false sense of freedom to say anything we want because we don't feel like we are truly addressing the person, nor do we feel responsibility for their feelings due to the technical anonymity of our sub-tweet. It's the newest kind of cyberbullying, and it's spreading every day because it's so easy. As we all know, it's addictive to be in on a secret, and to be in on a sub-tweet is exactly that.

For her thirtieth birthday, my then-girlfriend Gina wanted to throw a small cocktail party for her closest friends. Of course, we knew there would be people we had to leave off the guest list—once you invite any peripheral friends, the floodgates open and there are fifty more you're obligated to invite, and you might as well post the event on all of your social media for the entire public to see. After mulling over the endless lists of best friends, mutual friends, and obligatory invitees, we arrived at a sane number of guests. We knew that there would probably be four or five people who would be insulted to have not received an invite and would probably be disappointed when hundreds of Facebook photos were splattered across their feed, but we were happy with the list, and we went with it. The party was a huge success, and as we expected, our guests posted photos onto Facebook. As Gina and I went through the album, we noticed that one name reappeared in the comments section of several photos.

"Wow! What a great party, wish I had been there!"

"Everyone looks so beautiful. So sad that I missed it."

"Whoa. Looks like this night was a blast . . . Almost as much fun as we had in Cabo . . ." (Ellipses are always a sure sign of intense feelings, insecurity, or contemplation, and this comment had two sets of ellipses, so I am pretty sure this person was feeling terribly left out.)

The comments were made by Camille, one of Gina's high

school friends, who had narrowly missed the cut. She was one of the few we felt bad about (but not bad enough to invite her). Her comments on Facebook, however, reminded us why we kept her off the list: the truth is that she and Gina had been friends in high school, but this was fifteen years later and they simply weren't that close. If she felt close enough to the birthday girl to be invited to her thirtieth birthday and was hurt when she wasn't, perhaps she might have felt close enough to talk to Gina in person about it. Instead, Camille opted to make her point in front of the thousands of people (friends of friends) who could see the album.

Facebook and other social media provide a venue for people to express feelings without the consequence of an awkward in-person or on-phone response. It is easy to get in that first or last jab without having to feel embarrassed or defensive or to fear any repercussions. Like the boss who uses a human resources team to fire his right-hand man, Facebook, Twitter, and other social media sites have become mediums for the meek and cowardly.

Every impulsive statement and every irrational reaction seem to make their way onto the screen. Passive-aggressive tendencies and cruelty are magnified as impulse overrides our ability to contemplate what we really want to say and how it may impact the person we're "talking" to.

If we get into an argument, our typed responses overflow onto the screen, interrupting each other as we try to get our point across without reading the other person's messages back. We're not even thinking through what we are typing. In these heated, filterless moments, we are capable of easy, thoughtless cruelty. On the other side, the person we're fighting with may not even be reading our responses because they are clicking their own keys just as furiously. Often a fight that did not even have to happen—and would most likely not have happened in person—escalates into something much more damaging. As William Safire wrote in his former "On Language" column in the *New York Times Magazine*, "The pregnant pause has been digitally aborted."

Tone runs the very likely risk of being lost online. "When people tease or bully face-to-face," says Dr. Robin Kowalski, Clemson University psychologist and author of *Cyberbullying: Bullying in the Digital Age*, "they use off-record markers (winks, smiles, etc.) to indicate the intent behind their behavior and to assess its impact." But when we are online, hidden behind a screen, we miss these nuances. One can never tell if a sarcastic comment is truly sarcastic or if the writer is typing an actual opinion. We've lost the ability to read people. No matter how many emoticons we use, reading someone's words on a screen seldom allows us to fully understand that person's tone. It's hard to tell over text whether you are being teased or abused. This is part of the reason emojis have become so crucial to text talk. A statement that can read as mean or undermining gets much nicer (or harder to assail) with a little smiley face next to it.

My friend Keryn once told me that I should watch the nuances of my text messages because they often made transparent my insecurities. She told me, for instance, when I said something that I wasn't sure would be taken well or perhaps made a joke that I wasn't positive was funny or not, I always wrote *ha* at the end of the text. Even worse than that, I apparently was also utilizing the *ha* when I wrote something desperately insecure. *I feel like you're ignoring me ha* or *I should probably just go home I'm so hungover ha.* Now, reading it back to myself, it does sound insecure, and overwhelmingly so. We forget not only the indelibility of texting and posting but also how much of what we're trying to hide or project is blatantly obvious to everyone else.

So as we forget the implications of what we're writing, whether or not we're taking the time to consider the consequences of our actions, we're still acting with agency. We usually know what we're doing while we're doing it. I have posted photographs of myself with new girlfriends—and looking back, it was probably just to make my exes jealous and to show off how fabulous and better my life is without them. I wasn't being consciously mean-spirited, but I think subconsciously, I knew what I was doing. I knew it would be hurtful for my ex to see me happy with someone new. I have a friend who consistently posts photos of herself and a "celebrity" friend. Sure, they are truly friends. I know that. But they are not ten times closer than she is to her other friends, yet she posts about this particular friendship ten times more. I know it's childish and preening. But that's what we do to show the world and ourselves how happy and amazing our lives are.

After Brenda and I had stopped speaking, a Facebook war broke out. It was actually more of a cold war, because we never fought or spoke directly. We were both in new relationships but were still embittered from our breakup, and Facebook and Twitter were the perfect tools to make one another jealous. One of the things that had bonded us was that we are both foodies and always enjoyed going out to new restaurants or cooking fantastically complicated meals and posting pictures on Facebook or Twitter. This became the focus of our new war. One of us would post a photo and description of something we had just cooked for our new significant other, and within an hour there would be a new photograph of an equally complicated and tasty meal on the other's profile. I'd upload a photo of seared tuna with shaved truffles with the words "Fourth course at Eleven Madison Park," which would be followed a few hours later with Brenda's "Finishing my fifth course at Per Se—farm fresh eggs with thyme smoked prosciutto. Best meal EVER."

It was silly, competitive, and clearly pretentious. I could have avoided all this by cutting Brenda out, unfriending her on Facebook, or unfollowing her on Twitter, but I couldn't turn away; I wanted that access, just as I'm sure she wanted that access to me. I think we both also forgot how incredibly stupid we looked to our other friends and the rest of the world that was viewing us on social media. All either of us cared about was what the other saw; we were posting for each other. We forgot that others were still reading our posts and judging us. When I got engaged to the woman I'd later marry, naturally, I posted the news on Facebook. Four days later, Brenda posted that she'd gotten engaged. I had assumed our cold war was over. It had been so long that I don't think we were still tacitly playing the strange digital game, but that coincidence certainly made me think twice.

We would never dream of bragging out loud in person, but cloaked as a status update or tweet it's suddenly all right to self-promote, self-congratulate, and otherwise flaunt every nuance of one's life. The way we announce our relationships with one another is no exception. When Facebook offered its users the ability to declare their relationship status to their friends, a new sort of silent electronic dagger came into the world. People began to announce that they were "In a Relationship," "Married," or the dreaded "Single." This new rite of passage forces some undeclared couples to have a "state of the union" discussion. I've heard some people joke that if the relationship isn't posted on Facebook, it isn't happening in real life. And then there are the poor souls who learn about the lives of exes, crushes, or hookup buddies and ache with the grief of unrequited love. The potential for pain is massive.

My friend Kate had been in love with the same boy, Brandon, since college. Their on-again-off-again relationship had monopolized her emotional life since sophomore year. After graduation, Kate stayed in California but Brandon moved to Seattle with another girl who had gone to college with them but whom Kate didn't really know. Kate was devastated. She found solace, albeit the kind that keeps you awake at night, in the fact that Brandon said this relationship wasn't serious. He also came to visit every other weekend, staying with Kate as if they were boyfriend and girlfriend. They had nightly phone conversations (after

Brandon's girlfriend fell asleep) in which they mutually professed their love for each other and lamented the fact that they lived so far away. This went on for years. Either he had a crisis of conscience or a panic attack about his girlfriend finding out, and Brandon decided that he needed to end things with Kate. Five or ten years ago, he might have called her—or even met her in person—to break off their affair. In a worst-case scenario, he might even have written a long, tortured letter (or e-mail!) explaining that he couldn't betray the girl he hadn't expected to fall in love with but now found himself utterly connected and loyal to. Brandon didn't do any of those things.

It was a Thursday evening before the second weekend of the month, which meant that Brandon would be arriving in California the next day and Kate would have a boyfriend for approximately forty-eight hours. In bed, Kate went through her nightly Facebook routine—reading through her news feed, allowing her mind to wander the endless tangents of mutual friends' photos and wall updates. Then she got to Brandon's profile. She liked to look at his photos, and in the safety of the nonjudgmental confines of her room, she would dissect them, especially the few of him and the girl he had actually dismissed as a "casual fling." Brandon usually avoided posting photos of himself with the girl. (I had always believed he untagged them out of fear that Kate would finally realize that his relationship was far from casual and break up with him.) That night, though, as she arrived on Brandon's page, something was different. Kate noticed his new profile picture right away. The girl was in it. Four inches below that was the status update dreaded by any ex: "Brandon is in a relationship with Andrea."

Throughout her relationship with Brandon she had turned Andrea into a faceless and nameless nonperson. But as Kate clicked over to Andrea's profile, which was open for everyone to see, she found out where Andrea worked, that she had recently gotten promoted, that she loved the Rob Lowe movie *About Last Night* . . . Andrea was real. Kate felt almost guilty for looking, as if she were snooping, even though Andrea had made everything visible. And more than that, Kate finally had to accept that she herself was the other woman, and that the other other woman had won.

That night, for the first time in a year and a half, Brandon didn't call Kate to say he loved her. Perhaps he was avoiding her, as he knew she would have seen the new posts. When he arrived in California, he didn't head straight to her apartment, either; instead, he texted her to meet for the dreaded coffee. She agreed to go, if only just to confront this sudden turn of events. It turned out that he hadn't had the heart (or the guts) to tell Kate that things had gotten serious with Andrea but still lamented that she had found out through Facebook. What a liar. Brandon was completely aware, like any person under the age of eighty (it actually turned out that Kate's grandmother had found out as well—she liked to peruse Kate's mother's Facebook from time to time, and Kate's mother was also friends with Brandon), that if you post something on Facebook, the news will reach scores of people within minutes and everyone you know (and want it to reach) within two hours—especially if someone is looking for it, as he knew Kate would be. He had virtually vomited the details of his relationship all over his Facebook profile, making it embarrassingly obvious and impossible to miss. Brandon had let Facebook do his dirty work.

A graphic designer by the name of Lee Byron wrote about a poll conducted on Facebook that found that 75 percent of those born before 1975 broke up with significant others in person, while those born after 1984 are twice as likely to break up via the digital world. Further, a 2011 study by a market research firm revealed that 33 percent of people have ended their relationships over Facebook, text, or e-mail. We are relying on digital means—Facebook, Twitter, texting, instant messenger, Gchat—to avoid the mess of dealing with each other's emotions. An impetus for my writing this book, among other things, was that I was, in fact, broken up with via e-mail when I checked my e-mail at thirty-seven thousand feet in the air aboard a plane to Los Angeles. (I'll get to that shortly.) The Internet is full of wonder and possibility but it can also shield us from the dirty work of life, letting us unplug and power down any time we feel a little bit of discomfort.

6

I Didn't Mean to Do That

Texting and Facebooking and tweeting and Instagram-ming and e-mailing move at lightning speed and require a fast response. When we move quickly, we are often sloppy and make careless mistakes. Arguments get out of hand more quickly in text than in person, and as we Instagram, tweet, and update our Facebook statuses more quickly than our good judgment can control, our inadvertent and mistaken actions have consequences that can reverberate in our lives, even if they do give us plenty of fantastically hilarious stories to tell.

Nearly everyone I know has slapped their hand to their forehead or felt the pins and needles rising up in their body after the realization that they made a digital mistake.

As the writer of a book on this topic, I would be remiss if I failed to include the best (the worst) stories of accidental "liking," drunk texting, messaging the wrong person, and of course my favorite, the accidental reply-all. Below are my favorite stories in this category. All of them happened to someone I know and I apologize if you find yours here.

• • •

Let's start with something rather benign. When I was dating Samantha, I had a daily routine of checking Brenda's Facebook page. I liked to see what she was doing and mostly who she was hanging out with or (cringe) dating. It was harmless, albeit weak, but everyone I knew was guilty of committing the same crime, so I accepted my own weakness and stalked on. One night at dinner with Samantha and another couple, I felt a sudden urge to check Brenda's Facebook. Under the table, I managed to guide my fingers and navigate my phone to my Facebook app. I was so proud of myself for being able to do this blind—what a thing to be proud of! In my glory, I fumbled the next step. Instead of clicking the search button where I was planning to write Brenda's full name and click on her profile, I found myself in the "Update Status" box. I typed in "Brenda Taylor." Before I had a chance to peruse what I thought would be her Facebook page, the conversation turned to something pertaining to my work and I reengaged in the dinner, answering a few questions and forgetting about my stalking quest for the moment. A few minutes later, my phone buzzed. It was my friend Amy. *Kim—wtf are you doing on Facebook?* I had no idea what she meant but I was suddenly dizzy with anxiety. I looked down at my phone. My profile's most recent update, which appeared in every single one of my friends' feeds (including Samantha's), read "Kimmy Stolz is Brenda Taylor." I went into a panic and quickly deleted it. I think I got lucky because Samantha never brought it up. But I assume, given the frequency with which we all check our Facebook accounts, I shared my transparent stalking with at least four hundred to four hundred fifty friends during the ten minutes it was up before I managed to delete it.

* * *

I met one of my best friends, Nicole, while working at MTV. We were close for a few years before she met Dina, who would later become her wife. In the beginning of their relationship, they were long-distance, as Nicole lived in New York and Dina lived in Seattle. They and their long-distance texts were certainly hot and heavy. One late night, Dina texted something to Nicole, but Nicole had to put her phone away because she was at a work function and her boss had come over to have a drink with her. As soon as she got the chance, she found Dina's name in her iPhone and texted *I want to ____ you and then ____ you with ____* (there is really no more I can write without losing my book deal). A few minutes later, Nicole found that she had no response. Five minutes later, still nothing. So she opened up her texts to see what happened. Well, turns out the contact "Dina" was dangerously (a little too dangerously) close to the contact "Dad." She had sent her father an extremely racy text that would likely change her relationship with him forever (even if just from pure awkwardness). Nicole couldn't breathe. She found her friend Lauren at the party, who quickly brainstormed a plan to help Nicole. Lauren called Nicole's dad on his house line, which, thankfully for the believability of Nicole's story, was named "Home" in her contacts. Her father picked up. Lauren, masking her voice, said, "Hi, I just found this phone at a bar. Some people were messing with it but left it here and I don't think it's theirs. Is it yours?" Nicole's father bought the story (we think) and Nicole got away with seeming irresponsible to her father rather than like a guilty sexter. Nice save, Lauren!

• • •

When I was modeling, I was represented by a top agency (which was also an acting agency) that also represented some very famous celebrities (I was not one of them). Every so often, a great party would come up with a sponsor or organization that wanted some big names at their event for the press to write up. The biggest celebrities barely went, but the smaller ones (like me) went often (free drinks, great music, and a red carpet that we hoped would heighten our popularity—win-win-win!). Usually the assistants would send out the party invites and BCC the entire list of talent (you never know when SJP or Jennifer Lawrence might decide to randomly grace your party, and that is a big win— it's worth a shot). The e-mail would go out to thousands of people: talent, other agents, publicists, and of course press. One sad Sunday, however, one of the assistants at the agency forgot the most important part of the e-mail: to BCC. I remember sitting at my dining room table, opening up the e-mail, and suddenly having the personal e-mail addresses of everyone from Lindsay Lohan (think 2006) to Ben Affleck to Sandra Bullock to three of the Knicks to the entire Trump family! I never ended up doing anything with the list (though sometimes when I see one of their e-mails in my contact list I send them an invite to something like my dog's first birthday party just because I think it's funny), but I imagine some of the people on that list (ahem, members of the press) might have found it quite useful. Needless to say, the assistant was fired immediately, just minutes after her fingers touched "Send."

* * *

My friend Kelly dated a guy for five years after college. They had a relatively healthy relationship, albeit a tumultuous breakup. Not tumultuous in a Brenda kind of way but more the type of torrid love that just can't sustain itself, which almost always leads to drama and heartbreak. After they were unable to make a clean break, Kelly and her boyfriend finally decided that they would stop talking. It gutted them to do so, but it was the only way either of them could move on.

A few weeks later, Kelly started feeling anxious and panicked that her boyfriend had moved on (she never thought he actually would) and was dating someone else. While she was generally an extremely strong-willed person, the desire to check his Facebook was just too much to bear. So, she signed on and checked. His most recent update was surprisingly depressing. His grandfather had just died and he had posted a photo of him. She felt bad for him. She wanted to reach out and knew at some point she would, but later on, when someone actually gave her the news. She didn't want her ex to know she had been perusing his page, obsessing. She clicked to scroll down the page to see what else he'd posted. Click she did, but on the wrong *part* of the page. She clicked "like." Kelly had just "liked" her ex's grandfather's death. *Kelly likes this post*. Ugh. She tried to undo it but knew the notification would still pop up on her ex-boyfriend's phone and he would know that she liked the post. Not only would he know she liked the post, but he would know she was stalking his Facebook page. Panicked, she called him immediately but there was no answer. She was insecure and defeated; the last few weeks of being "strong" were erased and it was all because of Facebook.

. . .

My friend Clare landed a job the summer before we graduated college at a top NYC law firm. It was an extremely prestigious program that only accepted 5 percent of its applicants. She excelled through the summer and had even been comfortable enough there to come out and tell her coworkers and fellow interns (there were two hundred in all) that she was gay. During the course of the summer, she also managed to find another lesbian in the program—we'll call her Susie—who was out as well. They became great friends and even shared their respective crushes on the hot and successful female lawyers who were mentors and role models for the interns. Clare and Susie joked constantly about their schoolgirl crushes on Abby, an especially powerful lawyer, who mentored Susie. As the summer was coming to a close, the interns sent around a mass e-mail about what great present they could give Abby to thank her for being such a great mentor: gift certificates, Kiehl's baskets, even an amazing Balenciaga purse. Clare and Susie maintained their own e-mail correspondence joking about taking Abby out to dinner one-on-one on a date or buying her an apartment and cooking dinner for her there. Susie had replied-all to the two-hundred-person intern mass e-mail chain that perhaps a gift certificate for a dinner for two to Per Se might be a nice idea so that she could take her husband or friend or whomever she wished. People responded, liking the idea, and the conversation moved on to how they would split the purchase. Clare, aiming to get some laughs out of Susie, replied to Susie's e-mail, intending it to go *only* to Susie, saying something about wanting to be Abby's dinner date and hoping to make Abby fall in love with her, and then said some other, um, explicit things that aren't quite appropriate for this publication. About ten seconds after she hit "Send," Clare's phone was buzzing. Susie was calling. Confused, Clare picked up. She could only make out the term *reply-all* before Clare realized what she had done. She had sent her schoolgirl-crush fantasy about Abby to the entire group. She had replied-all instead of replying to just Susie. Before long, she was called into an HR office (of course one of her fellow interns had ratted her out—how else do you get ahead!?) and her summer was terminated one week early.

• • •

My friend Tina had just started hooking up with a new guy. She was excited! But she was also twenty-two at the time and was falling victim to frequent drunk (and very late-night) texting. The lucky guy's name was Jack, and while the relationship was far from serious, she liked hanging out with him (usually between eleven P.M. and three A.M.). One night around one A.M. she was feeling especially anxious to see Jack, and in order to entice him (in case he was home or didn't feel like going out) she wrote some rather racy text messages, hoping that it would be enough to get him to come see her. After an embarrassing twenty-five-minute waiting time, a text came through. It read: "Tina. Stop booty calling your forty-year-old married COUSIN Jack. Seriously this has happened several times now. I'm sure Jack is great but I'm certainly not him. Change one of our names in your phone, please." Tina was mortified. She quickly learned from that experience to always include last names with family members and lovers so as not to write inappropriate texts to people, namely our parents and family.

• • •

One of my colleagues, Erin, played volleyball at college. For years, her team felt mismanaged and somewhat mistreated by their coach. By Erin's sophomore year, the seniors on the team decided it made sense to send an e-mail out to the team discussing the best way to stand up for themselves and all of the terrible things their coach had done. At the end of the e-mail, the seniors asked each person on the team to write back an example of the type of behavior or a specific experience they wished to address with the coach. E-mails were fired back and forth about everyone's worst experiences and what they hated most about their coach. Apparently, one tiny mistake occurred during the e-mail transaction. The coach's name was Carrie Walsh, similar (too similar) to one of the players, Carrie Wallace. In one of the seniors' haste, her Gmail auto-filled the "To:" field with "Carrie Walsh" (the coach!). Twenty-six e-mails later, the entire team realized that they had just been sending scathing e-mails about their coach *to* their coach. The next day, Coach Walsh called a meeting with the entire team. She made the seniors read aloud all of the e-mails and effectively stopped the team from being able to meet with the athletic director or take the matter any further. It was a terrible start to another terrible season.

* * *

One person's devastating humiliation is another person's chuckles. It's all LOL until it happens to you, and then sometimes it takes years of deep therapy and repentance before you can even crack a half smile about your embarrassing Internet fiasco. No matter how careful you are, no one is immune to digital mistakes and snafus. And when we're texting and e-mailing and posting 24/7, it's hard to keep in mind that once you post something on the Internet or send something to someone else's phone, it lives forever—and is completely out of your control. Including incriminating photos, drunken texts, and poorly thought-out tweets.

Of course I can't deny the fact that these things can also

be good. We can get in touch with old friends. We can meet significant others. We can share videos of puppies singing and playing the piano. Worldwide awareness of current events and new developments in the world of art grow and social movements and political agendas gain momentum. We can rally together in the name of what we think is right. The Arab Spring started because of a tweet; LGBT kids all over the country got stronger and braver because of a You-Tube campaign called It Gets Better.

But for every one of those connective and electrifying movements, there's a deep well of humiliation waiting to be stumbled into and a load of mindless, unimportant drivel that steals our attention and distracts us from what is real— and when I say *real*, I mean where you are sitting or standing right now, where you exist. Your actual real life.

7

Unfriending My Ex

S o that breakup story I mentioned . . .

Well, one morning a few years ago, I sat on a plane bound for Los Angeles. I was relaxed. I had spent the previous night with Tracy, my girlfriend, and despite some rough spots in the previous months, things were good.

I opened up my laptop and accessed my e-mail and was surprised to find nothing from her—no message wishing me a good flight or sending her love, which she would usually send without fail. I sent her an e-mail, expecting a quick reply in return. Four minutes passed. No response. Around the fifteen-minute mark, panic set in. I wrote a note to my friend and roommate Kelly and asked her to check up on Tracy by sending her a text and seeing if she read it. She kindly did as I asked while I waited, thousands of feet in the air.

About fifteen minutes later, an e-mail from Tracy popped onto my screen. That fateful moment will haunt me (and my Gmail inbox) forever. Tracy hadn't written anything, only forwarded a recent (intoxicated) e-mail conversation that I'd had with my ex-girlfriend (*see:* Brenda, from previous chapters), in which we lamented that we missed each other and "wished we could go back to the beginning." Brenda and I had been in touch sporadically since our breakup, and there were obvious romantic overtones to this e-mail chain. You see, Brenda and I would decide to stop speaking for a period of time. Our lives would go back to normal and everyone would be happy until one of us hinted at missing the other via Facebook, Twitter, Friendster (it was still a thing then!), or a Gchat status. By "in touch sporadically" I mean that we were not actually speaking or texting much at all but consistently stalking each other and sending subliminal messages via social media. Brenda and I had been in one of our out-of-touch stages for nine months or so until about a week before my flight. I was in a bar with friends and on a bathroom line, I decided to check my Twitter feed. There it was, glaring in my face: "BrendaDC: Even if you were a million miles away, I could still feel you in my bed . . ." A lyric from "Try Sleeping with a Broken Heart" by Alicia Keys—it was a song we'd both listened to during our out-of-touch periods, and it always reminded us of each other. My heart sank. I knew I wasn't strong enough to ignore it. When I got home, I posted a video by the same artist on my Facebook page. This could mean one and only one thing to Brenda: I missed her too and I wanted to talk. Two days later we were e-mailing again. Three days later I forwarded the entire e-mail conversation to my roommate Kelly, begging for advice, or maybe just so I could admit my wrongdoing to *someone*, albeit not to the person I should have. I had forwarded it to her because I just needed to share it with someone. I felt terrible. Of course, Tracy had opened Kelly's computer to check her own e-mail, and as my luck would have it, Kelly's e-mail was open and Tracy was able to see my entire e-mail exchange with Brenda. There I was, thirty-seven thousand feet off the ground, realizing that an e-mail I had written while inebriated to an ex-girlfriend that had been inspired by a tweet followed by a Facebook status had cost me my relationship.

One of the many things I could not get past, and part of what motivated me to write this book, was that I knew I would not have made the same mistake—I would *not* have contacted a former girlfriend—had smartphones and social networking sites not granted me an easy way to act on a dangerous and damaging impulse. I was to blame, I was guilty, but Facebook, Twitter, my iPhone, and e-mail were my accomplices.

Recently there was a little meme that went around Instagram and Facebook that said: "If you think your relationship is real, just trade phones for a day. No Passwords. 90% of you will be single again." This little provocation got so much heat because it's true that our phones are where we live out a lot of our private lives. And they are filled with temptation. So no matter how much a person intends to stay faithful, the combination of fantasy, impulse, and accessibility (and sometimes booze) keeps the e-cheating train moving. I once heard that couples should always keep "locks" or "passwords" on their phones so that the urge to check up on each other could not be indulged. I come from another school of thought. My wife and I never once put a lock on either of our phones. Sure, in the beginning of our relationship, we both broke down a few times, asked to see texts, or checked up on each other, but to this day neither of us keeps secrets from each other. It just isn't worth it (and I would like to think that when you find the person to spend your life with, you won't have any secrets, though perhaps this is naïve). After some time, we didn't feel the urge to check each other's phones anymore. Because, you know, we grew to trust each other. Sure, maybe we got to the trusting place in a strange way, but it's a 2014 kind of way, and it worked. From my past experiences, however, and from talking to my friends and family, I think our open-phone policy may have been in the 1 percent.

Perhaps the digitally acquired ADD impels us always to search for the next-best thing, making us more willing—and able—to do so. Maybe we feel like running at the first hint of boredom, and the easiest way to go is often to the Facebook page of an ex or a crush, where we can avoid wallowing in whatever present doldrums or misery we find ourselves in and escape into a happy universe based on reality but subject to all kinds of flourishes of the imagination. It's easy to riff on what you see onscreen and develop romantic feelings for people you're really not all that connected to in reality.

My friend Molly (not a *90210* character) told me once that being in love is not an actual feeling but a state of mind: you are in love with the *idea* of being in love more than you love the person you're with, and the relationship endures because you *grow* to love that person. I think today this is more true than ever. When we meet someone, we can find bits and pieces about them on their social media, even if we haven't "friended" them yet. We can let our minds embellish and exaggerate the parts of their personalities that work for us. "Wow! She likes the Knife! She must also like Hot Chip and MNDR and Haim! She's perfect for me!" Before we know it, we are thinking about the types of kids we could have together and where we might spend our honeymoon. The person we are "stalking" is putting their best foot forward (or what they think is their best foot) and we are running with it, connecting the details of their Facebook pages, Twitter feeds, and Instagram uploads to make them our perfect partner. We fall in love with the idea of them, not who they truly are, on the Web, where there are endless opportunities to interact with an endless number of willing partners. The Internet—and all of the people you might meet there—never shuts down. The door to impulsive action is always wide open—whether it leads to innocent fantasy or more devious affairs. All of the exes you would have lost touch with in the predigital age are now just a click away. It's never really over. It can begin with little notes, a simple "like" on a status update or two, a few flirty comments on a wall . . . reaching out to someone else only takes one push of a button, so it doesn't involve the same degree of premeditation or agony as a face-to-face meeting might entail. It's easy to dip your toe in and see what you get back. The stakes are low. If you don't get a response, no big deal.

The Internet not only stirs temptation but also provides opportunities that can be dangerous for relationships. A friend of mine said, "People are more accessible than they once were. If you were to cheat before the existence of cell phones and Facebook, it was much more deliberate. Now we are in situations that seem socially acceptable and it is often too late before you realize it's not. It can all happen super quickly." I found it so much easier to slide into my virtual affair with Brenda because we were doing it through the written word—through texts, e-mail, Twitter, and Facebook comments. It started out completely casually and before long I was on that slippery slope.

It's not like cheating didn't exist pre-Facebook. But it's undeniable that our impulsivity has been heightened with these tools. My friend Emily, an NYC-based musician, says that she never would have cheated on her ex-boyfriend had current communication technology not existed. Her boyfriend Todd was her band's drummer, and the two of them hired a producer, Dylan, to work on one of their albums. After many long days in the studio getting to know each other, and what seemed like harmless flirting, Emily and Dylan started texting sporadically. One night, she received a text from him that said, *Feeling totally conflicted about having the hots for you.* Emily was drinking at my house and, coincidentally, was on a break (they had many) with Todd.

(By the way, I totally subscribe to the Rachel argument in *Rachel vs. Ross*—yes I'm talking about the television show *Friends*—that it is still cheating even if one is on a "break.") The argument, her anger, the booze, and her phone drove Emily to write back almost immediately with *meet me on 14th n 2nd*, and the rest is history. "I never would have called Dylan on the phone and invited him over," she said. "And if this were 1995 and I had called him on a *landline*, he never would have been home anyway. So if not for texting, that night wouldn't have happened."

After a week of cheating on Todd with Dylan, Emily realized she needed time to figure things out. She told Dylan she was taking a month off from talking to him, and over the next few days, they refrained from speaking or texting. Thanks to the Internet, however, Dylan was still present in her life, and the allure of mysterious messages sent through Twitter and Facebook proved to be too difficult to resist. "I knew that every tweet he posted was like a secret message to me," Emily told me. "He would tweet lyrics to songs we had listened to together . . . He would send coded messages that no one would understand but me, and through them, he wasn't violating our no-contact agreement while I cleaned up the mess with Todd." The secrecy of their messages, hidden in plain sight, made everything sexier and heightened the sense of romance. Although Emily might have eventually ended things with Todd, her texting and tweeting with Dylan expedited her breakup as well as the initiation of a new and lasting relationship. I remember another time when Emily sat at my house debating whether or not to text Dylan. After a long debate, we decided that she should. She asked him where to meet her; he said he would meet her "anytime anywhere." So naturally, they chose the Upper East Side, near my house. I attended their wedding last summer. So sometimes there is a happy ending to the "illegitimate" text. Just . . . not often.

Dylan might not have texted Emily, and Emily might not have had the impulse to reply so easily, without the relative safety and distance afforded by their screens. Certain words—especially if they are words that make you vulnerable—are more easily typed than said aloud. It could be said that this is a good thing—that texting and e-mail allow us to do and say things that we do not have the courage to in person.

But it's also true that the speed and recklessness with which we are able to send our most impulsive thoughts allow temptation to overtake reason with an unhealthy frequency—particularly when combined with alcohol. Most people I know admit to sending drunk texts to an ex (guilty); about three-quarters regret sending those messages, and I suspect that those who don't probably don't feel guilty because they didn't happen to get caught (or had a really great night, or have no conscience). Alcohol certainly lowers our impulse control, but when we are digitally connected, we don't even need alcohol. We can lose out to the temptation to make our fantasies a reality even when we are sober.

More than one person I spoke to described all of this communication as a "slippery slope." Are we cheating if we "like" an ex's post or photo? If we only have a "tex-tual" relationship and chat over Facebook, IM, or text? If we follow an ex or crush on Instagram or Twitter? Aaron Ben-Zeév, PhD, reviews various elements of the argument in his illuminating article "Is Chatting Cheating?" Appar-ently, anything we do online—chatting, meeting, or just sending the occasional text—could be harming a relation-ship. "People consider their online sexual relationships as real, as they experience psychological states similar to those typically elicited by off-line relationships." According to those he spoke with, if one partner isn't aware of what the other is doing, "it's cheating as it involves deception." And because of that one simple factor, all the partners he inter-viewed agreed that there should be no distinction made be-tween online and off-line affairs. Even if one doesn't cheat physically, it doesn't lessen the fact that they've betrayed the relationship. The problem that a lot of couples face is that one partner doesn't see an online affair as cheating be-cause it occurs in an "imaginary" realm, but Dr. Ben-Zeév concludes that "since online affairs are *psychologically* real they often cause actual harm to the primary, off-line roman-tic relationships."

During my sophomore year of college, I was in a short but strangely serious relationship with a girl named Valerie, whom I had met on my rugby team (yes, I played rugby and, yes, I get the cliché). A few months into our relation-ship, I got back in touch with a friend from high school who had recently come out of the closet. Her name, inci-dentally, was also Valerie. (For the purposes of this story,

I will to refer to these women as Valerie1, my girlfriend, and Valerie2, my paramour, even though that is *not* how I referred to them in real life, in public or private.) I began to spend more and more time thinking about Valerie2, and soon enough we were sending texts to each other throughout the day. The messages weren't flirtatious per se, but I began to disclose details about my life that I should have been sending only to Valerie1. When Valerie2 came to visit me at college about a month after we became reacquainted, the texts, IMs, Gchats, and e-mails began to intensify, and what had once been easy to qualify—to myself—as an innocent and friendly correspondence now took on a tone that was obviously romantic and sexual. And as any cheater knows, electronic communication leaves a "paper" trail: Gmail saves conversations, IMs are stored in hard drive folders, and a simple search on a smartphone can retrieve all conversations related to a certain name. Of course, today, we have apps like Snapchat that appear to be designed for the cheater, or at least the person who wants to avoid any type of saved "history." Nearly everyone I talk to who has cheated on someone in the past few months, upon hearing my panicked concern that they are going to get caught, responds, "Thank you, Snapchat," or "That's why I use Snapchat," or something about owing their life to Snapchat. But isn't Snapchat just making things worse? If we were impulsive enough to make mistakes on history-saving mechanisms like e-mail and text, we are triply so on a non-history-saving app like Snapchat (also, I bet all of those Snapchats are saved *somewhere*). Actions have consequences, whether they are recorded on your text stream or not. At some point, if the affair becomes serious enough, whether via Snapchat, text, e-mail, or Facebook, more avenues are going to be used. Maybe you can conduct a one-night stand on only one medium. But anything beyond that gets more complicated. We are humans. We get sloppy. We leave "paper" trails.

Since Snapchat didn't exist when I was maintaining my double-Valerie life, deleting conversations, finding folders, and running computer-wide searches for all traces of Valerie2 became part of my daily routine. Each attempt to cleanse my sins by deleting my Web history, chats, and e-mails made me feel even more paranoid and guilty. I deleted Valerie2's number, e-mail address, and made myself invisible on Gchat, and told her I had to take time away from her. I even named her "NO" in my phone to remind me not to contact her. Despite this, all it took was a weak moment, and it would dawn on me that Valerie2 was a simple click away. Sending an "innocent" text just to say hello or an IM telling her I missed her was all too easy. Over several weeks, I deleted and recovered her number and e-mail address so often that I eventually memorized both, and texting her would only take seconds to act on.

The beginning of the end of my relationship with Valerie1 came to a head one night when I left my AOL IM open on my computer while I took a shower (I was in college, and at the time AOL IM was still alive and breathing as a way to communicate). I had, of course, taken every precaution to delete any incriminating evidence of my textual relationship with Valerie2—but I didn't think of everything. With timing that only karma could deliver, my friend Lisa—one of the few people to whom I had disclosed my transgressions—started an IM with me by writing, "Hey Kimmy, just saying hi. How are the Valeries?" Valerie1 happened to be checking her e-mail on my computer, while I was taking a shower and was front and center to see Lisa's IM. Girlfriends always tend to know more than you think they do, and Valerie1 had previously expressed concern about how close Valerie2 and I had become—an inquisition I had survived and successfully put an end to. But the four words "How are the Valeries?" were enough to confirm the suspicions my girlfriend still harbored. It took me three weeks and a complete suspension of contact with Valerie2 to finally right things with my girlfriend. The relationship was damaged, though, and we broke up a few months later.

• • •

The Internet dangles endless options and temptations. Of course there is a plus side: we can discover new interests (like online book clubs and meet-up sports teams—I'm really stretching to find something positive), and it allows us to stay in touch with old friends we may have otherwise lost track of. But it also can create a false sense of closeness. We may begin to feel a connection, because we have bonded in some way, mentally or emotionally, over something moving or humorous. We both like the same cat video. We both agree that the craze for Lady Gaga is overdone (we must be the only ones in the world who feel this way!). That shared bond, no matter how small, can be enough to make us *feel* that we have feelings for someone, when it is just a *state of mind*. When you can connect with someone through text and e-mail and social media, it is so much easier to build yourself up into a lather about someone than if you were just maybe running into that person on the street and then going on with your day without seeing the person again. In real life, that person might have had something in her teeth or she might have been wearing Uggs. But online, you're seeing her on her best day, from her best angle, and you're bonding over your shared love of Sour Patch Kids or *Breaking Bad* or dry white wine. These seem to you like the first mini-seeds of love. But more so than in real life, you're not loving a person, you're loving the *idea* of the person that can be nurtured and tended in your mind. Turns out Molly was on to something.

Given that it's never over and the long list of ex-crushes, flings, and serious relationships is always just a click away, we must practice self-control. But sometimes we can't help ourselves. My own ability to get over and move on from relationships has been slowed by the fact that these social networking tools keep the images and details of these people in my mind. As a friend admitted to me, "I would be able to move on from my past relationship more easily if it weren't for Facebook. I can see what my ex-boyfriend is up to in a way that I otherwise would not. I can see his day-to-day activities. It's addictive and it sucks."

The constant access to potential, current, and even past lovers in various ways can spur certain hopes within us.

Anything can trigger our impulses to attempt a reunion. My friend Jesse started dating Nikki at the beginning of one summer, and by the next, they were living together and quite serious but going through a bickering stage. One evening when we were hanging out, Jesse told me he missed the simplicity of single life and that he felt emotionally drained by his relationship. I told him this feeling was not uncommon in relationships and that he should push through it, especially if he loved Nikki. His patience was clearly waning, however, and one night after work when Nikki had a late dinner meeting, he found himself on his ex-girlfriend's Facebook page, looking at her recent photos, wall posts, and status updates. On the news feed, he noticed a fateful update from the week before: "Gabrielle is now Single." The spark of interest, along with the revelation (thanks to a recent "Summer Fun" photo album—I have yet to see a "Summer Fun" album that isn't asking for an ex to see it and get jealous) that Gabrielle had a new attractive haircut, was enough to ignite a fantasy about what Jesse's life would have been like had he not broken up with Gabrielle or ever met Nikki. I had always considered Jesse an uncomplicated guy who would not be caught obsessing over any girl, so it surprised me when he told me that over the next couple of weeks he spent between thirty minutes and an hour each day poring over Gabrielle's Facebook profile, checking her updates and posts obsessively to see if any of them included new men.

One night, after an argument with Nikki, Jesse decided to write Gabrielle a Facebook message. Gabrielle responded, and one message turned into two, which turned into approximately seven or eight back-and-forths every day for several weeks, at which point Jesse came to me in a panic. He was completely surprised by how quickly his online reunion with Gabrielle had progressed and realized he would have to break up with Nikki if he was going to let it advance any farther without completely going against his conscience and values.

Whether Jesse was already cheating at that point is up for debate; nevertheless, it had taken just one click of the mouse to get in touch with Gabrielle—one click that helped escalate Jesse's feelings. He broke up with Nikki and told her that he just needed some time to be alone and that he was not mentally ready to take their relationship to the next level—not 100 percent true reasoning, which was soon publicly exposed when Gabrielle posted photos from the first night she and Jesse finally hung out. Nikki, of course, had friended Gabrielle early on in her relationship with Jesse (she figured, *I must friend Jesse's ex! Keep my enemies closer . . .*). Jesse was not aware of their Facebook friendship and Gabrielle had forgotten about it or didn't care. Nikki was crushed and Jesse found his clothes (which he had been meaning to pick up) outside his old apartment the next day.

But the twisted game of social media wasn't over. It wasn't until a few weeks later, when Jesse found out that Gabrielle had actually gotten back together with her boyfriend—but had neglected to let him know or update her Facebook status—that he realized how much he had allowed himself to get carried away. Jesse's obsession and imagined life based on what he saw on Gabrielle's Facebook profile had led him to believe their connection was much stronger than it actually was. It's easy to forget, but we actually *do* have a choice about what we post, and Gabrielle's editorial decisions had fooled Jesse. In reality, she had been seeing her ex-boyfriend and had decided to get back together with him. She may have been using Jesse to make her boyfriend jealous; no matter what, Jesse lost this game of Facebook Fantasy.

Some lawyers are calling Facebook the "marriage killer." Mark Keenan of the UK-based website Divorce-Online.com, which allows men and women to file uncontested divorces, scanned the documents filed on his site and found that 989 of the company's 5,000 most recent divorce petitions contained the word "Facebook." Upon further exploration, he found that Facebook had actually been a stated factor in approximately one in five divorces filed on his site. Back on these shores, the American Academy of Matrimonial Lawyers announced that 81 percent of its members had seen an increase in cases using evidence from social media sites over the past five years. The same study found that Facebook is the unrivaled leader in providing online divorce evidence, with 66 percent "citing it as a primary source."

The Internet isn't only dangling the temptation of new relationships, it's also stoking doubt and suspicion in our existing ones. Even when we're in happy, functional relationships, almost all of us check up on our significant other via e-mail, Facebook, or Instagram at least once. I talked to a few people who even admitted to hacking into their significant other's account more than three times a day. One person told me that when she found out her boyfriend's password, she checked obsessively. All day, every day. "It was as if I couldn't help myself," she said. "One day I sat down in my dining room and read every e-mail he had sent or received over the past two years." Another person told me, "I regret doing it every time—and will probably do it again tonight!"

In her online column on the *Psychology Today* website, Dr. Pamela Haag details a study called "More Information Than You Ever Wanted," which demonstrates that Facebook and other social media sites "enhance jealousy" in relationships. Essentially, the site keeps us in a "romantic jealousy feedback loop." On Facebook, partners are privy to information they might not have previously discovered, which has the potential to incite jealousy. The jealousy then leads to more significant surveillance, which can expose even more jealousy-inducing fare. Dr. Haag mentioned that some consider Facebook surveillance to be addiction as well. The people who admitted to me that they have hacked into their significant other's account or looked through their phones aren't crazy. Relationships put our hearts on the line, and the possibility that we can either confirm our fears or rid ourselves of worry by simply clicking a mouse or unlocking a phone proves irresistible for most of us.

My friend Colin had an interesting experience with snooping while on a break with his longtime girlfriend Donna. Colin and Donna had been dating on and off (and by "on and off" I mean that they broke up and got back together at least thirty times in three years). During one of their breaks, Colin signed on to Match.com. He figured now was as good a time as any. He needed a clean slate and Match.com seemed like the safest way to get it. One day, Colin was "winked" at by a girl who in her photo bore an extremely close resemblance to his ex Donna (the photo was a little blurry but tall, brown hair, and skinny were enough to spark his interest). *Great*, he thought, *just my type (in looks anyway!)*. He winked back. He signed on a few days later to see if this hot Donna look-alike had made the next move. Indeed she had. The girl had written him a message. Excited, he opened it up to find just two words: "Fuck You." Turned out Donna had discovered perhaps a new and somewhat nuanced way to stalk one's exes, via a dating site. Sadly for Colin, Donna not only flicked him off via Match message, but she screenshotted his profile and sent it with a scathing message about him to everyone they knew. One of their main reasons for breaking up in the first place was a lack of trust, and now Colin's attempt at safe and anony- mous dating had become dangerous as well. He closed his Match.com account the next day.

The fact is, even if two people fundamentally trust, love, and care for each other, the little machines that bind us together and provide us with so much information and access have made us more suspicious, controlling, and easy to manipulate—and that can be immensely damaging to any relationship. I have been on both sides of the fence— obsessing over details on a girlfriend's Facebook page as well as feeling like my social media accounts were under constant surveillance. There were times when I allowed my imagination, insecurity, and paranoia to take over my (not always incorrect) thoughts. The use of text and other smartphone technologies like WhatsApp and Snapchat can cause increased suspicion and irrational thoughts because they make secret messaging easy. We wonder why our friends and significant others are reading our notes but not writing back, or why our messages aren't getting through. I can remember the times when I've said good night to a girlfriend before she went to sleep, then sent a quick "I love you!" and watched as the message didn't go through. Paranoia abounds: *Who could she be talking to? Who would her last phone call of the night be to—if not me? Am I being cheated on?* These feelings and questions, while irrational, are altogether common.

On the other hand, being monitored is no walk in the park. When I was with Brenda, I felt so closely watched that I felt the urge to delete even the most innocent of texts and e-mails. They just weren't worth the discussion. My urge to delete so as not to discuss was actually one of the worst ideas I ever had—because one day, my texts to a friend didn't quite line up. Brenda could tell I had deleted something and even though I was truly doing nothing wrong and had just deleted a selfie my friend had taken to show me her new dress, I looked like a criminal. Four hours of fighting and convincing later, I realized I should have just kept the texts there. No one likes a deleter. So truly, on both sides of the coin, it's not a fun game. You feel either suffocated and monitored or jealous and panicked. Without social media and smartphones, instead of dealing with those terrible feelings, you might just be watching old episodes of *Twin Peaks* together (or *The X Factor* or *Modern Family* if you aren't still rewatching a David Lynch show from 1990 like me).

In a way, social media has made us all snoops—suspicious because we're all aware that the potential for cheating is just a click away. Knowing how easy it is to find out about another's deception by checking social media profiles, text histories, and e-mail logs can breed a very real compulsion. But it doesn't feel good to snoop. Best-case scenario, you learn that your boyfriend or girlfriend's slate is clean—but the suspicion still doesn't subside. And because we feel compelled to keep checking, it's creating a whole new way to cheat, even if our partner isn't. The fact of the matter is that even if nothing is found, the simple transgression can ruin a relationship. A good friend once told me, "I have been the victim of the dreaded hack-in. I left my e-mail up once and my girlfriend went through everything and questioned me about over sixty e-mails. Even though there weren't any instances of infidelity [on my part], the complete lack of trust and invasion of privacy caused our relationship to be tainted and ultimately end."

Knowing that temptation abounds can also make us—or our partners—hungry for more control in our relationships, which can be just as detrimental. An MTV initiative called A Thin Line, which is aimed at preventing digital abuse, found that more than one in ten people have had a boyfriend or girlfriend demand passwords, and more than one in ten people have also had a significant other demand that they unfriend or unfollow an ex on a social networking site like Facebook or Twitter. Sometimes, people will even force each other to "friend" an ex so that the ex can see the person happy and joyful in a new relationship. It's backward but it happens. The quest for transparency in our relationships can be suffocating.

Carly, one of my most mature and levelheaded friends, had a breakdown because of Find My Friends, an app that, according to the site, lets those who are connected see where their friends are located geographically. Carly and her boyfriend had been in a long-distance relationship for five years, and they found that each knowing where the other was and being able to picture each other at work, the store, or the gym made them feel closer in a way. Over time, however, Carly found herself becoming less rational when it came to the location obsession Find My Friends had ignited in her. She said, "I found myself using it several times throughout the day to casually check and see what Aaron was doing . . . One night, we got into a silly fight and ended up not speaking the next day. Unbeknownst to him, I followed him all day via Find My Friends to see what he was up to: office, doctor, meetings, etc. By the afternoon, I was pretty upset that he had not tried to contact me. I figured he was busy and would text me when he got home. I checked the app around seven P.M. and saw that he was at a hockey game. I texted him saying, 'Happy to see you care more about a sports team than you do about my feelings.' I text-screamed at him until I eventually saw (through Find My Friends) that he had left the game and gone home before the first period had even ended." Aaron broke up with Carly a few months later because he felt she had changed and that her recent tendencies to be "crazy" and "controlling" had ruined their relationship. I was upset to hear this but not surprised; the digiverse has left a pile of relationship rubble in its wake, breaking up even those couples that had previously seemed quite solid. Carly had been pretty normal before social media, but Find My Friends had turned her into a crazy and suffocating girlfriend. Like the BlackBerry Messenger and iPhone read receipt notifications—and most of the access we get through social media sites—the app provided too much information and planted seeds of doubt where there needn't have been doubt.

We can blame Facebook and other social media sites for our transgressions, but there does come a point when our personal demons take over. Across the world, there have been some very extreme cases in which Facebook has ruined not only relationships but entire offscreen lives. In one story I read, an off-duty cop checked up on his wife's online profile and found that she was having a flirtatious exchange with one of his friends. He confronted the mutual friend, punched him in the face, and ripped his shirt. The cop ended up on administrative leave and was later charged with battery. His story is benign compared to that of a young woman named Sarah, twenty-six, who was stabbed thirteen times by her estranged husband after he checked her Facebook page and found that she had changed her relationship status to single. The couple had split four days before the murder. Just last year, a Philadelphia man stabbed his wife because he was angry that she "liked" someone else's post on Facebook. Another woman ended up dead after she changed her relationship status to "single" and announced she was leaving her husband by posting on her wall. Her husband allegedly saw the status update and murdered her before killing himself. And finally, a long-distance relationship between a man in Trinidad and a woman in London turned deadly after he found a photo on Facebook of her with another man and went to London and murdered her. Although these stories are clearly extreme, they point to the irrational feelings and rage that we can feel from learning information through social networking sites. The jealousy, embarrassment, and anger caused by seeing items on an ex's Facebook profile (or any social media site) can lead a generally sane and levelheaded individual to emotional breakdown and incite fights, the breakup of friendships and relationships, and in some cases, physical harm and death. With the exception of these dramatic cases, for most of us, the worst-case scenario is that through snooping, our fears will be confirmed. Elissa, a journalist from Manhattan, told me, "I hate that I checked my boyfriend's e-mails, and I hate that when I did, my fears were confirmed, because that meant I will always check his e-mails from now on."

Many believe it is their *right* to peruse their boyfriend or girlfriend's e-mail accounts, phone, and Facebook accounts, arguing that "only the guilty have something to hide," and if someone wants to keep them out of their business, they must be hiding a secret lover or budding flirtation. My friend Laura told me, "I don't think people should be snooping but I also think there is a clear problem if some- one won't let their girlfriend or boyfriend look through their phone once in a while."

I've been in relationships with exceptionally private people, and their privacy made me wonder whether they were deceiving me. I tend to leave my e-mail account open and logged in all day long on my home computer, and I have never had a lock on my iPhone. The only times I've made sure to sign out of my own accounts were when I was actually hiding a conversation that I did not want my significant other to read, so someone's intense desire for pri- vacy and diligence in signing out of online accounts makes me nervous. On the other hand, I have dated people who are careful to sign out of their e-mail and Facebook and are always sure to have a password on their phones; I would venture a guess that many readers are thinking that these exes were most likely hiding something from me. I learned, however, that some people are more private and their desire to keep their e-mails and social networking accounts secret has more to do with their values and less to do with their actions.

Certainly, Facebook provides some advantages in the personal and professional arenas of life. Some people I spoke with even said that Facebook has had a positive effect on their relationships and helped build trust and intimacy. We now know more about the people in our life—what they are thinking about, what amuses them, and who they are hanging out with, as well as what they are doing and with whom. Sarah, a twenty-nine-year-old from Maine, told me, "There is definitely that element where you feel you need to reveal more to your significant other about who wrote on your Facebook wall or who tagged you in a photo . . . Perhaps we become more faithful in our relationships because of this." While it's true Facebook and the digital media world do in a way make us more accountable and can call us out on our transgressions, so many of those transgressions are initiated because of Facebook itself.

A rainy Sunday of meaningless Internet exploration can turn into a full-fledged stalking session. Feelings of rejection that we thought we had moved past can be reanimated by simply clicking through a friend's Facebook album. Those who have broken your heart reappear through Facebook pages, Twitter feeds, and chat statuses. You can unfriend and unfollow but they are always there, connected through other individuals we actually want to hear about. We may forget them, but then a little one-word comment can remind us they exist, sending us reeling into our romantic pasts.

For those of us who remember a time when these outlets did not exist, we took for granted that after breakups we could erase our exes from our lives and never accidentally (or on purpose) come across the details of their lives. Now we have access to everything. And unless we delete our accounts and disconnect our lives, we will continue in the paranoia-and-jealousy loop, continually checking our significant others' e-mail and fighting because of what we find on Facebook.

How many times have I told myself I'm getting off Facebook? The truth is I'm never getting off Facebook. Even though we hate so much of what it yields, we'll continue to hack in, cheat, and fight, for one reason: we can't stop.

8

Does This Filter Make Me Look Famous?

> I was meant for reality television. I'm
> going to be famous if I keep tweeting.
> People love my shit, seriously.

T he words above were spoken by Teddy, a thirty-one-year-old Long Island–born gay hairstylist with whom I had become friends through work. He could not sing, dance, or cook. He was not athletic, nor was he particularly good-looking. He was not funny, nor did he possess any particularly unique knowledge. The most interesting thing about him was that he was potentially the worst speller I had ever met. The only reality show on which he had a shot of being cast was Bravo's (now defunct) hair competition *Shear Genius*, which he denounced as "not good enough," claiming that no one had ever come out of that show and become *truly* famous (even though Tabatha Coffey, the winner from season one, got her own show and earned a place in reality show history). I asked Teddy what show he would be on, if he could choose; he said he thought there was a lot of interest out there for a show about his *own* life as a celebrity hairstylist and that he was working on a pitch to send around to "the networks."

I first thought Teddy was joking around, but after spending more time with him I realized he was serious. Teddy was someone who had always wanted to be famous—I think he became a hairstylist just so he could be closer to celebrities—and I wondered if he would have worked so hard at it or aspired to that particular kind of fame before the advent of reality television or Twitter.

All of our friends knew that there was nothing about Teddy that would ever draw an audience. After all, we were in a post–*Queer Eye* age, so he was about six years too late for any producer to place him on a show merely because he was gay. (I got "lucky" when I was cast on *America's Next Top Model* because lesbians were far less prevalent on reality television in 2005, and putting one in the midst of a dozen aspiring female models was still considered "interesting.") No, there was nothing about Teddy that would convince anyone that he was "made" for reality television, and yet he believed wholeheartedly that it was his destiny and made it his life's passion and long-term goal—even more than helping celebrities and regular humans look fabulous.

Teddy was resolved to make fame a reality. He was a Twitter star in his own mind; he once held a contest among his fans (he did not have any fans) to give $100 to his one thousandth follower. Around 405, he made it $100 for his five hundredth follower. One week later, he owed $100 to his aunt Jenny. But Teddy didn't give up. He truly believed he could "make it" by remaining "in touch" with his celebrity acquaintances and getting them to retweet his posts and @ him on their own. Despite the fact that his tweets and updates weren't even mildly compelling, he did not hesitate to declare at every opportunity that he was more interesting than other outrageous reality stars. It was nice to see one of my peers so positive and full of hope for his future, but it would have been more heartening if he'd had some legitimate aspiration beyond having his unremarkable persona put on a pedestal by a television platform. Teddy's fantasy seemed to me like a narcissist's wet dream.

But what do the professionals say? The *Diagnostic and Statistical Manual of Mental Disorders* (*DSM*), the bible of the psychiatric profession, defines people with narcissistic personality disorder as not only grandiose in their actions and statements (*I was meant to be on reality television!*) but also having a dire "need for admiration" and a "lack of empathy." As Dr. Elias Aboujaoude explains in *Virtually You*, "DSM-certified narcissists usually believe they are 'special and unique and can only be understood or should associate with other high-status people.'"

Forgive me for playing armchair psychologist, but Teddy's behavior corresponded with this diagnosis: his constant tweets, his off-the-charts self-concept, and his belief that he should only hang out with celebrities, those whom our superficial society put up on a pedestal. In general,

Teddy's use of social media was, if anything, amplifying his condition.

Dr. Aboujaoude argues that the number of people with narcissistic disorder has increased in recent years as the Internet fosters some of the characteristics that typify the personality disorder. Whether it is due to something inherent in our psychology or to our nonstop use of social media, most of us post and tweet and update seeking admiration and affirmation. We yearn for—and expect—others to look at us, to comment on our posts and reply to our texts. This never-ending loop feeds self-obsession; we *require* the attention to satisfy our narcissism, and so we share more, becoming even more infatuated with our display and how others will see us.

I said good-bye to my quick stint on reality television in 2005, but in some ways I feel like I'm still living on a reality show. This time, however, we're *all* contestants. Sure, one could say our lives have always been a performance—adjusting our behavior in school, at work, with family and friends—but never before have we had our thoughts, actions, and images aired in a public place, preserved for posterity. Suddenly we're rewarded for acting on impulse, and that impulse is to share—and we do, in a constant stream of texts, status updates, Vines, tweets, Snapchats, and Instagram posts. Now, more than ever, we want people to pay attention to us—to follow us, like us, comment on our posts, and retweet our thoughts. We gauge what is appropriate and acceptable by what we see on television and our overflowing social media feeds. Like reality TV contestants, we wheedle and overshare in our desperation to stay in the limelight. We reveal more and consider consequences less.

Social media makes us hyperaware of where we stand in the sphere of social competition, and we're constantly trying to calculate according to unwritten, ever-changing rules who is the most popular, how we're getting along with our significant other, or if we're good people—because just like the television version of this reality competition, we can get kicked off, lose friends, and alienate people. In a strange electronic version of survival of the fittest, the social media reality game show we're all playing is about not necessarily how many friends we have but how we rank in our own minds and how secure we are in our relationships. We may have scores of friends but still feel lost and lonely (as many do), also so many of us ramp up our attention-grabbing revelations just to feel like we're still doing okay.

One of the advantages (and disadvantages) of being on a reality television show is that you suddenly become part of a little club. Whenever you see another person who has been on reality television, for better or worse, you are instantly connected. I had a brief but intense "friendship" with a girl who'd starred on a popular reality show. We'll call her Nikki. We traded stories, tweeted at each other, and talked about the opportunities we had or hadn't gotten since our stints on reality TV. As time passed and our friendship developed, I began noticing some red flags.

She met most of her friends on Facebook, Twitter, and Instagram. They were all her "fans" who constantly tagged and @-ed her. They made her feel famous and didn't mind being the minions who trailed behind her as she swanned into restaurants or bars. The minions felt special for hanging out with someone who had been on television, and she felt popular, but more important, she "looked" popular to everyone else. As weeks turned into months, the revolving door brought an onslaught of new "friends," none staying more than a month at a time. (It's tough being a minion!) New week, new posse. Her ability to make a brand-new acquaintance look like her best friend on social media was astounding, even impressive.

We were on the Lower East Side one night when Hotel Chantelle had just opened. We were walking by after leaving a dive bar on the corner and heading to the deli to get sandwiches before going our separate ways. We walked past the long line to get into Hotel Chantelle, where some people recognized Nikki from television and asked to take a photo. Neither she nor I was a stranger to this occurrence, but I was surprised at what happened next. My phone started buzzing in my pocket. Facebook, Twitter, Instagram alerts abounded! "Just leaving @HotelChantelle with my girl @ KimmyStolz and met a fan on the way out!" Nikki had fabricated our night right in front of me. Our trip to get a sandwich had suddenly become a glamorous escapade. And then came more buzzing from Nikki's phone. Her fans were tweeting back and Instagramming comments like "OMG I LOVE NIKKI" and "OMG how do I get to be in your shoes for a day."

As time went on, I began noticing that when we hung out, she would suggest we do strange things for photos so that we could "post" them. We stood on cars (why? It looked kind of cool), we rented scooters but barely rode them anywhere (so many photos, so little time!), and we went to recently opened, exclusive restaurants where I ate half the menu and she barely touched the food but made sure to photograph my food and then Instagram it and tag it so that people knew she had been there. I stopped talking to Nikki a few weeks later. I understood the desire to pump up your life on social media to make it look like you're having a better time than you are or to post a photo of yourself and a celebrity you love because you want to tell the story to your friends. But Nikki had taken it to levels that made me cringe.

Years later, she was arrested for drinking and driving (I literally mean drinking and driving: she was holding a beer while driving her car over the Manhattan Bridge). How did she get caught? A nearby cop noticed five or six flashes in the car (Nikki always made sure to take five or six or twenty photos before posting anything—it was important to look her best). The cop pulled her over and arrested her for drinking and driving, and texting and driving. She had it all! She tried to take down the photo of her holding the beer while driving a day later (after her release from jail) but it was too late. She had uploaded it just before getting pulled over and all of the bloggers she had friended on Facebook (to enhance her public image, of course!) had already uploaded it to their own sites.

We may not all have the same kind of platform or aspirations as Nikki had, but whether we realize it or not, we are *all* putting on a show, using social media to expand our social circle or mold how the world sees us. We revamp our online personas with selective status updates, check-ins, and Instagram photos, in order to control how we are perceived by those in our digital circle. We try to prove that our lives are *amazing*, that we go on *amazing* adventures and eat *amazing* food with our *amazing* friends. The goal is to appear as happy and successful and good-looking as possible. Bit by digital bit, we have become obsessed with and addicted to sharing so as to get any reaction that proves people are interested in what we have to say. We have become a generation of oversharers, hyperaware of what we post and desperate for acknowledgment and affirmation.

Five years ago, I might have been compelled to share with a friend approximately one out of every one hundred thoughts passing through my head. Today, I find myself wanting to Instagram (which links to my Twitter and Facebook and Foursquare) about almost every experience or "interesting" place I go. But I also try to filter. I take a few seconds to read what I type and imagine how it will appear on someone else's feed. I try to share only what I think will make my followers happy—what is funny or interesting or strange—but I am aware as I do this that I am considering my image and the persona I want others to see. I am also aware that I fail at this "filtering" more than not. I fall victim to the desire to show off my amazing vacations or how amazing my weekend is out in the Hamptons with my family or how amazing my friends are. I hope some of my followers and friends have read up to this point in the book so I can apologize for some of my most shameless posts. I'm sorry, guys.

I always assumed that those who were not raised with all these digital tools would not feel this same urge. I was wrong. Since my mother joined Facebook, I've seen how it's grown to be a larger part of her life. One day, on a beach in Florida, we were watching in awe as spinner sharks swam just ten feet from the shore. "This is so amazing. Oooh, I wish I had my phone on me so I could put it on Facebook!" my mother said to me. I found it fascinating that Facebook had infiltrated the way she perceives the world and processes her experiences, just as it had mine eight years before. As the years have gone on, I've watched my mom become more and more immersed in Facebook and her desire to post the best photos of me, my wife, my dad, and our dogs. She commented recently that she had a lot of longtime friends over for a yearly get-together. And she noticed with some sadness that whereas in years past, they'd spent time gossiping and catching up over cocktails, a lot of the time they spent together, they were immersed in their phones, their various Facebook accounts, and respective games of Words with Friends.

• • •

Sharing as much as we do fosters the belief that our lives are just as interesting and compelling as those of people who are paid to be interesting and compelling—and that people want to hear our every thought and see pictures of our every meal. (How else to explain the innumerable mind-numbingly mundane tweets?) Our lives online give us a skewed sense of self-importance and a faulty perception of what's interesting about who we are, what we do, and what we think. If I see one more Instagram of a cartoon kitten, I'm going to have a breakdown. And please don't get me started on the inspirational quotes people are now posting instead of photos. Posting a photo of Bob Marley or snippet from a Robert Frost poem does not inspire me. It makes me hate you.

People believe they are projecting the best aspects of their personality when they post, upload, and tweet. But in real life, you are exposing yourself for what you really are: a puddle of raw and desperate insecurity. For instance:

- Picture of yourself with a celebrity? *I am in the "in" crowd and I'm at the highest social tier.* This translates to the reader as: you have never been friends with a celebrity and it took a great deal of awkwardness to get this photo.

- Any quote about achieving your dream? *I am in touch with my emotional side and I am successful because I believe in myself.* When I see these, I think: *You're unemployed.*

- Bob Marley quote? *I'm a hippie and I'm laid-back and very cool.* More like: you're a white kid who smokes weed.

- Robert Frost quote? *I'm highly educated and I "get" poetry.* Reads as: "The Road Not Taken" is the most overquoted poem in the history of mankind and you probably have never read the whole thing.

Dr. Aboujaoude explains that the virtual world changes how we see ourselves, so that we have "an exaggerated sense of our abilities, a superior attitude toward others, a new moral code that we adopt online, a proneness to impulsive behavior, a tendency to regress to childhood states when faced with an open browser." We post every thought that crosses our minds, resulting in a constant dialogue with the outside world and a relinquishment of the filters that once stopped us from embarrassing ourselves or boring others. The need to cultivate an audience—to win more followers—that social media facilitates, the delusion that we can all be stars, the pressure to share, the ability to do so instantaneously, along with the dissociation from reality—all of this fuels the making of our celebrity in our own minds.

Was it the advent of Facebook and Twitter (or even Myspace and Friendster, RIP) and the photo-based Instagram and SnapChat that ignited a narcissistic need to make our lives an open book (or news feed) for all to see? Or do these sites merely allow us to unleash the exhibitionistic, attention-seeking animal that until now has lain dormant inside of us?

Who knows the answer to this chicken-egg conundrum? One thing's for certain: my generation is the first one to come of age with the ability to Google ourselves and create online footprints. In a sense, the Internet made us all microcelebrities, and as much as some of us claim to despise it, it makes us feel special, because someone—anyone—has been paying attention.

We have always been obsessed with celebrity, but the

steady stream of blogs, gossip sites, and celebrities' own Twitter mumblings exacerbated the preoccupation. Then, as reality television shows became popular in the late 1990s and took over the television industry in the 2000s, we watched our peers grow (almost) rich and (very temporarily) famous from Myspace pages and YouTube videos. Slowly but surely, all of us—celebrities included—became our own mini reality-show machines, addicted to checking texts and tweets, sharing too much in order to gain any sort of affirmation that people cared. Nobody wanted to be left out. We may not be clinically diagnosed narcissists, but as Dr. Aboujaoude noted, the Internet is bringing many of us closer to it every day. And the more we're online, the more narcissistic and fame-obsessed we get.

Our social media feeds grant us a platform. The more people retweet or comment on our posts, the more entertaining and interesting we think we are. Coupled with the onslaught of reality television—where normal people become famous for just being themselves—we now all believe that we can be stars.

With the constant audience comes the pressure to perform. There's an art to being a social media star—there's a fine line that we have to walk, between giving the audience exactly what they want and becoming either a laughingstock that people want to forget or the boring or annoying character no one wants to be. You must be open to sharing but not weak enough to overshare. You want to post just enough so that people are intrigued by what you have to say and keep coming back, but not say too much or say things so often that they can predict what you're going to write or get bored and think, *Oh my God, not another tweet from Kim about her dog or another rant about being stuck in traffic on the way to Bridgehampton.* Ugh, I hate myself just typing this.

It used to be that when my friends and I were getting ready to go out, as we tried on outfits, put on our makeup, and discussed how we looked, we'd talk about who we hoped to see or hook up with that night and whether or not we looked good enough for the girls and guys we had crushes on. Today, however, the subject of the conversation has shifted. We talk about how we will look in the *photos* that will no doubt be posted onto Instagram or Facebook that night or the next day. We grab each other's phones, reserving the right to reject bad photos and unabashedly begging for an immediate upload and tag of the good ones. We used to want to look good for our potential hookups, our friends, and even ourselves. Now we strive to look good for Facebook or Instagram and just hope the people we *want* to see it are checking their feeds. If we are going to a party with paparazzi, we pray that some official photographer will be there to record it so that we can screenshot their photo the next day and upload it to our own Instagrams. If we think we look horrible, our mantra for the night will become, "Please don't tag me!" We are now more consumed with how the online world will view us than we are with the opinions of those whom we spend time with in person.

Since we're all just one viral video away from our own show and line of hair care products, we've not only become more self-obsessed, but we're also getting more judgmental about how other people are stacking up. We gauge others' looks, personality, wits, talent, and style compared to our own because, God forbid, they might make it before we do. I was once close with a girl who was on *The Real World*. She was very popular on her season and she and I had just about the same number of followers on Twitter and Instagram. We were both somewhat "edgy"-looking to the passerby and (you guessed it) we were both gay. It was just a year or two after I had been on *America's Next Top Model* and I was working as a model signed with Ford and as a VJ at MTV. She was just finishing her stint on *The Real World* and already had a contract to sign with CAA, a top acting agency, and she was talking to Fuse, MTV's competitor, about hosting a show for them. Remaining popular and in the public eye were massively important for both of our careers. I remember checking my Facebook and Myspace and feeling a lump in my stomach and a brush of panic every time I saw her post a photo of herself on a red carpet or with other celebrities. It was wrong and it reminded me of being one of the best players on the basketball team in sixth grade and being secretly angry and jealous every time my best friend scored. (Sorry, Liz!) Every move was competitive and we were vying for . . . well, I don't know what, but it certainly felt like we were vying for something major. I remember judging her outfits and being ecstatic when she finally got the job at Fuse. If it wasn't going to be Fuse, her next stop could have been MTV! MTV was *mine*. The truth is, of course, deep down I was always proud of her when she accomplished something, but it also struck a negative and panicked chord with me. We weren't close enough friends for me to feel selfless. I wanted to win, to have the better image, to get the appearances, and if she had to lose in order for me to achieve that, then so be it. I know she felt the same about me. So we judged each other silently (or sometimes with our friends—okay, fine, or sometimes with the entire MTV newsroom). But we were judging each other for things that we were guilty of doing as well.

This happens to all of us each day on Instagram, Facebook, Twitter, Vine, and all other forms of social media. We judge other people for their annoying, boring, oversharing, irrational, angry, or embarrassing posts, when most of us are writing the same kind of thing. We are judging everyone else, so we must be aware that people are judging us, and yet we drop ourselves in the fishbowl so willingly.

We are so desperate to succeed in our social media reality game show, and part of doing that is showing our best side—even if that means we have to lie. One night, I was composing a tweet about being out with my friends, choosing every word carefully. Of course, I knew that the tweet was for one purpose only: to make the ex who had broken up with me (but who I knew was still obsessively looking through my Facebook and Twitter feeds) think that I was doing okay—better than okay. She wasn't very good at hiding the fact that she compulsively perused my social media. I would post a photo of me and a friend (who happened to be extremely good-looking), and I would get a passive-aggressive text within thirty minutes; I would upload a song and she would tweet lyrics from the same artist. We were absolutely terrible at masking our inability to get over each other. But still, she had broken my heart and I wanted to show her that I had moved on, so I tried to make my night sound exciting and free. In reality, I was sitting at a dive bar with two friends, all of us bored and trying to figure out where to go next. I was actually planning my escape so I could go home and watch *Arrested Development*. Moments after I sent the post—something provocative like "another crazy night with the girls"—into the Twitterverse, the friend to my left pointed her phone at me and called me out on my pathetic lie. "Really, Kim?" I was embarrassed. Nothing shamed me more than coming across as the desperate girl attempting to contrive a tweet for someone who had cheated on her more than three months before. But a week later, I caught the same friend in a lie herself: she got into a fight with her boyfriend and tweeted that she was going out late, even though I had really just driven her home at eleven thirty P.M. This childish behavior is easy to cast aspersions on from the outside but surprisingly hard to avoid when it comes to our own online avatars.

No matter the motive—romantic, professional, or otherwise—we are increasingly turning to our social media sites and profiles to influence the world's perception of who we are. We can't help but tweet little lies and exaggerations, irrational in the belief that we will not get caught. We continue to share, attempting to convey one persona or project one emotion, even—or especially—if we are feeling the complete opposite.

• • •

So back to our favorite narcissistic hairstylist, Teddy. For three years I watched him on his quest for reality-show fame. I observed how he tried to become friends with every celebrity whose hair he touched. His record wasn't altogether bad actually: he generally became "friends" with one out of twenty and badgered several of them into tweeting at him at least once, a major accomplishment for him because it led to more followers, and the more he gained, the higher his chance of success—or so he told me. He tweeted at least fifteen times per day, and no less than fifteen of those tweets were either at a celebrity, an upload of a photograph of him standing with a celebrity, or the mention of a celebrity he had just "worked with," was about to see, or was "in touch" with. Judge Teddy as you may (I did), but he's not the only one doing this kind of thing. Of those I spoke with, around one out of every five people said they had a fifty-fifty chance of getting famous online. Fifty-fifty!

Our perception of our ability to achieve fame—and sustain it—is extremely skewed. *So You Think You Can Dance, The X Factor, America's Got Talent, American Idol, The Voice, Project Runway, America's Next Top Model* . . . there are vast TV empires that are built around the conceit that anyone can make it. As we share more and more online in an infinite attention-seeking loop of display and interaction, we're all producing our own little reality shows. Who's the hottest? Who has the most friends? Who did the best, most original thing last weekend? The judges are our friends. They've got the power to "like" or retweet a post. And as we keep the tally of the tens or twenties or hundreds of people who like what we're doing, what we're wearing, how we wore it, how we said it, where it happened, our egos become larger, and we delude ourselves into thinking that our lives are worthy of 24/7 documentation—and even worse, that our self-worth is based on the attention we receive online. In reality, very few of us will garner lasting fame by way of the Internet.

I found a list (online, of course) of ten people (and one cat) who became famous on the Internet in 2010 thanks to YouTube videos, tweets, or blogs. The amazing thing was that in spite of the fact that only a few years had passed, I recognized only two names—Antoine Dodson and Justin Halpern, who writes *Shit My Dad Says*. By the time I finished the final draft of this book, neither of those names rang a bell either.

If there are ten people who became famous through their Twitter account, and only two of them have name recognition that has lasted more than a year, then isn't it irrational that so many of us think that there is greater than a fifty-fifty chance that we will make ourselves famous simply by writing a blog, creating a YouTube channel, or putting an @ sign before our name? We convince ourselves that we can get famous through YouTube because Justin Bieber did it— ignoring that he not only had some talent but also *serious* luck when Scooter Braun came across his page.

Whether we yearn for actual fame or are just playing

at it through social media, we must be aware that the emotional and mental benefits we might potentially achieve from this exposure are not sustainable and not necessarily real. Unlike actors or musicians, who enrich people's lives with their talent and whose fans grow with their careers, reality television stars are generally famous because they did something insane or silly or even idiotic. They have a different fan base, perhaps a less sophisticated one than the likes of Jack Nicholson or Meryl Streep. The fame comes quickly and is concentrated in social media. It feels overwhelming and exciting but it ends just as quickly because there is generally no "talent" to carry one's career (and thus fans) any farther. According to Dr. Wicker, "The self-esteem boost that one gets from instant fame is artificial and externally based. It is not the individual discovering his or her own worth through self-exploration . . . It is an emotionally dangerous place to find self-worth." When the reasons we value ourselves are not based on our true accomplishments or true relationships, we can find ourselves in a precarious place if the attention ultimately slips away. In one year we can go from red carpets, $5,000 appearance fees, and constant looks and stops on the street to having trouble getting into the same parties and clubs we were once paid to appear at. I remember in 2006 when not a day went by without someone saying something like "OMG top model!" or "You were my *favorite*" to me, and today there are sometimes weeks in between occasions when someone spots me, and the intervals get longer and longer. When you're famous for a minute (or fifteen minutes), you think the sky is the limit. *I can be an actress! A musician! A television host! I can be Anderson Cooper!* But then a year later, you cringe at the fact that those things seemed attainable, especially since you can't act or sing, nor do you have any experience in broadcast news.

I was lucky to have other hopes besides being on a reality show. I had dreams of foreign policy think tanks, writing articles for publications I respected, and Wall Street, not Hollywood, paparazzi, and screaming fans. My nonchalance is the reason I survived my fifteen minutes (mostly) unscathed. The fact is that reality television, in its essence, is meant to build you up and break you down at the same time. It makes you feel like the current trajectory of your life pales in comparison to what you could achieve if you won the show's competition or at least finished close to the end. You begin to feel like you are already famous and celebrated by a large portion of the TV-viewing public. You begin to believe that you were meant to become famous and that you have finally landed on your life's right path. You become delusional in the belief that all of your new fame-filled dreams are achievable and within arm's reach. I had never wanted to be famous, nor had I wanted to be a model (I tried out for the show after I lost a bet to my friend Allison in college), and yet sometime during the third or fourth week of filming I was convinced that being a famous model or celebrity of any sort was necessary for my (short-term) happiness and sense of self-worth. I was sucked in. I wanted that life. As I advanced in the competition, that external boost of self-esteem—from the judges, the photographers, and the cameras—made me value myself on very superficial levels. It was not based on what I truly thought of myself or what I was really proud to have accomplished in my life. (Looking back on it now, it's similar to the addictive feeling of seeing hundreds of people "like" or retweet my posts on Facebook, Twitter, or Instagram.)

After being eliminated and returning to my life, I was able to recognize that my *Top Model* experience was interesting and exciting but not something that would make or break my life or any career that I went on to have. After I was through with *ANTM*, I swore to my friends and family and to myself that, no matter what, I would never do another reality television show. I look at how others fared and know that I have been truly lucky.

If people recognize me on the street and know that I was on *America's Next Top Model*, they generally remember that I was the "gay one" on the show, or that I got in a tussle because of a *granola bar*. No one remembers my runway walk (at least I hope they don't), nor do they remember my photos. Those "talents" just aren't what *Top Model* focuses on and therefore are not what the young women on the show are known for. If we remember faces or names it is usually for some unacceptable behavior that would get a normal person tossed out of a job.

Not having a skill does not seem to concern men and women like Teddy, who are desperate for worldwide recognition. They are not counting on putting their talent to work to get rich and famous. They do not want to be celebrated for their actual skills—they believe their skill is being *themselves*. This type of fame is unlikely to come to fruition and if by some odd chance it does, it almost always ends shortly after it begins.

Ironically, the most dangerous fate for someone like Teddy, whose whole life is engineered around trying to be famous, may be to actually achieve his goal and get his own show. The fall from grace and the loss of fame are tough on former reality show stars. After all, the kind of celebrity that comes from reality TV seldom lasts longer than a season or two. On the show, overinflated hopes of fame temporarily take flight before brutally crashing to the ground; they are where a person's fifteen minutes (or episodes) of fame converge with expectations of a future but instead are subject to the world's ADD, which quickly moves on to the next season's cast. The term *celebrity* is stripped away as quickly—and unceremoniously—as it was painted on. Bombarded and saturated with images, videos, and news about certain reality stars, we wait patiently for the star to burn out and fade away—as they all eventually will.

Despite witnessing the wreckage of several formerly famous individuals, however, we cannot deny the power the prospect of fame wields: we long for the affirmation. And so we continue to share more and more thoughts and pictures that we would have considered too private (and perhaps too shameful) to share only a few years ago.

Teddy is now almost forty and has just under a thousand followers. Where others judge his continued tweets @-ing celebrities as pathetic, he celebrates each one as progress.

9

Baby Steps

Are we all turning into cyborgs? Are we morphing into mechanical creatures who hide behind screens, unable to spend four minutes in quiet contemplation? As Instagram has surged in popularity, I wonder if our ADD has gotten so bad that we can't even focus on 140 characters anymore. So much less work to glance at a picture.

So, like, what are we supposed to do? I might complain about how lame Facebook is, but I'm still on Facebook. I "need" it. I need it. We are all attached to a digital umbilical cord. Jobs, friendships, education, and relationships are all maintained (and some would say *exist* or even *are created*) by way of this medium, which provides unprecedented communication tools for almost every objective. Keeping a job generally requires being available twenty-four hours a day, seven days a week. When I spent a week without my smartphone, I missed more than a few job opportunities because I was not readily available.

We have been infiltrated to the point that in February 2011, the SAT college entrance exam featured an essay topic on reality television programming, proving that even the College Board—which champions education and literacy and functions as the gatekeeper to higher learning—cannot deny its presence. The question read as follows:

> Reality television programs, which feature real people engaged in real activities rather than professional actors performing scripted scenes, are increasingly popular. These shows depict ordinary people competing in everything from singing and dancing to losing weight, or just living their everyday lives. Most people believe that the reality these shows portray is authentic, but they are being misled. How authentic can these shows be when producers design challenges for the participants and then editors alter filmed scenes? Do people benefit from forms of entertainment that show so-called reality, or are such forms of entertainment harmful?

Students, parents, and teachers revolted in unison, saying that the question was unfair for those who do not have televisions or who had not watched enough reality television to be able to answer the question as well as those who did. There was also concern over whether the college board was setting a bad example and advocating the watching of so-called trashy shows like *Jersey Shore*, *Real Housewives*, or of course *America's Next Top Model*.

The salient point here is that reality shows have so insinuated themselves into the fabric of our lives that they are *part of our standardized testing*. Having an opinion about reality shows determined whether this cohort was going to be matriculating at Harvard or sweeping the floor at their local Starbucks.

. . .

So what are we supposed to do about the addiction, the distraction, the desperation for fame and acceptance, the narcissism, the loneliness and cruelty—to once again become empathetic individuals who can think and operate in an offscreen world? This might sound sort of hokey, but I guess the question I'm left with after thinking through all of this stuff is: how can we become more human?

I came across a few words from Erik Qualman, author of *Socialnomics* and an expert on digital trends. He said, "We don't have a choice on whether we *do* social media, the question is how well we *do* it." Qualman articulates what I have been feeling: that we are forcibly bound to this technology, that it is here to stay, and that if we are to succeed in our lives and relationships, we need to learn how to use it *responsibly*. Trying to engineer a life entirely devoid of smartphones or the Internet is completely irrational and unrealistic and kind of Unabomber. Our world has been forever altered by social media and the portable devices that we have become so dependent on, and yet we must still find a way to make our lives, relationships, and careers work *within* this new norm. We must find a balance between our interpersonal relationships and our technological ones, and we need to learn how to use these devices mindfully.

Even if we have been using these interactive platforms for years, in the larger scheme of things, we are all beginners at this. So much about the way we think and communicate has changed in so little time. And where we are now with regard to smartphones, social networking, and reality television is a relative hiccup in the face of the changes we will see over the coming decades.

In my quest to find some concrete solutions, I looked to the past. Before I got my smartphone—when I could still focus—I loved to read novels, books about history, and all kinds of articles. I would compare where I was at the time to the people I was reading about, knowing we can always look to history for a set of experiences that mirror our own and try to learn from it.

Please allow me to be a nerd for a minute. In a sense, we can consider ourselves to be living through a new industrial revolution, and our dilemma is mirrored in that of the Luddites, a community of British textile artisans who protested during the *first* industrial revolution, which took place in the eighteenth and nineteenth centuries. The Luddites were named after Ned Ludd, a guy who, in his dismay over the way machines were taking over his craft, smashed a mechanized loom. He called for a return to a way of doing business that predated the technology that had created so many social and economic changes and had left so many of his friends and associates without work. The Luddites burned down factories, handloom weavers, and cotton mills. The government responded by making "machine breaking" a capital crime and sentenced many Luddites to death by execution. The Luddite movement ultimately failed because its proponents fully and completely rejected the changes occurring within society.

There were some factory workers who, while also suffering lower wages or lost jobs, just as the Luddites had, took a different approach: they adapted to society's new landscape and learned how to operate machinery. Some were even forward-thinking enough that they were able to see the positive impact that the industrial revolution would ultimately have on wages, production, and the economy.

From these men and women, as well as from the failure of the Luddites, we learn that we cannot totally reject smartphones, social media, texting, or reality television. A complete and total disavowal of the technological realities our digital age has produced would most definitely end in defeat . . . or at least sad irrelevance.

We can't hate on our smartphones or our social media any more than we can say electricity or automobiles have destroyed the fabric of our society. Candlelit dinners and bicycle rides are enjoyable activities, but anyone who thinks we can go back to a world without cars or electrical power is delusional. We can't wish away reality. If we logged off of all types of social media and digital communication, we would miss out on a crucial aspect of the human experience.

William Powers, author of *Hamlet's BlackBerry*, told me about a teacher who explained that every time she tried to keep social media out of the classroom or teach students about the importance of face-to-face communication, she would get a call from parents worried that if their kids stopped using social media, they would have no friends and be incapable of networking and getting jobs. I'm sure these parents don't want their kids to turn into Internet zombies, but they've got a point: few who completely forgo the digital world are going to be able to be fully functioning members of the workforce and society.

Still, we can do more to connect in person . . . with people. In writing this book, I expected I would be able to reduce my Internet and smartphone addiction. Or at least I hoped that my digitally acquired attention deficit disorder would become milder. I thought that by writing this book, I would find the willpower to make changes and become a more efficient and focused individual.

I was mostly wrong but a little bit right. My iPhone is still the first thing I check when I wake up and I feel panicked if more than six hours go by without my checking Instagram. I still find it hard to enjoy a concert or a day at the beach without posting *something*. And it is more than likely that you found out about this book because of some aspect of social media. I have no doubt I will be Instagramming, tweeting, Facebooking, and Tumblring about it daily.

I didn't want to feel as if I were utterly alone in my failure, so I asked William Powers if writing his book about the perils of technology helped him at all with his addiction. "That is the one thing that has surprised me," he told me. "I thought that after writing the book and being so public with it that I would get to a place where it would be better for me. It hasn't. That said, there is solace in knowing that so many other people have this issue—our whole culture is addicted, basically. This made me feel both better because my book maybe helped someone, but also worse in the sense that I'm really worried about where we are going." His admission reassured me (kind of).

Countless articles and books tell you that you can lose weight by taking special pills or limiting your intake of x, y, or z food products. Some are making the same kind of insane promises to fix digital addiction: I even saw an article recently saying that you could solve Internet addiction *in three easy steps that take no effort from you*! I did not bother to read the body of the article because it harkened back to my dieting days, and I know how that ends (no skinnier). The solution won't come in a bottle.

As Powers told me, "The digital future is not just about taking time off from your screen, but also *being thoughtful* about how technology has evolved . . . You need to realize that you can shape your own life no matter how tethered you feel in this digital world." What does shaping your own life really mean? To start, we can begin showing up for meetings and dinners with friends without our hands and eyes constantly on our phone. We can give people we're actually with our full attention in the moment we're actually with them. We can do our best to show up for our everyday lives.

Here is what I've resolved to do: make more phone calls. Make an effort to call at least one friend a day, to set up a date with them, and when I meet them in person, I am going to put my phone away. Perhaps I'll even arrange Skype calls or video chats, so I can see my friends' faces and hear voices rather than just reading *hahaha* or gauging tone via emoticons.

I work in a face-paced environment where there is a lot of yelling and orders are given left and right, but before I come home to my wife, I have to change my mind-set, reclaim my compassion and patience. I am able to do that because I am aware of the difference between the two atmospheres. I think we have to learn to do this with social media as well. There is the terse, somewhat distracted, everything-happens-at-once world of social media interaction, and then there is the slower, more focused human-to-human interaction. With an overabundance of social media, we act like our social media selves when we sit down to dinner or attempt to read or do work. My phone lights up constantly with texts, e-mails, Instagram, Twitter, SnapChat, and Facebook notifications, and even CNN and Seeking Alpha alerts. When I go to dinner with a friend, I cannot stop this from happening. What I can do, though, is try to slow down, focus on what's in front of me, and keep my phone out of my sight.

. . .

My wife deactivated her Facebook account not too long ago, and she is infinitely happier. She didn't want to be inundated with a stream of updates from people whom she didn't care about. Who cares if that girl from your second-grade class loves rice pudding or is excited to see what's going to happen on this season of *SYTYCD*? She wanted to live in the present and the future, not the past. I envy that.

My wife's good-bye to Facebook also benefited me; I've been relieved of the impulse to see what's happening on her page since she doesn't have one. In turn, while I link my Twitter and my Instagram to Facebook, I barely spend any time on it myself. I (almost) never peruse the pages of the people I once knew or dated. If we were both still active Facebook users, we would probably fight more, as we would question each other's every move. Finally, and perhaps most importantly, we have more time with each other.

In a *USA Today* interview, Rolling Stones front man Mick Jagger admitted, "I spend way too much time on the computer and not enough time playing the guitar . . . There's an underlying problem of this screen life taking over all of your life." The day after he read that, my best friend's younger brother quit Facebook so he could "focus on the guitar."

Arianna Huffington, who founded the political blog (and subsequent online empire) the *Huffington Post*, spoke out in 2010 about how our nation's leaders are failing us because of their own overconnectedness to technology. "Look at the bad decisions our leaders are making," said Huffington. "I have to believe it's because they are hyper-connected to technology, and not sufficiently connected to their own wisdom." Huffington's comment reminded me of what Ralph Waldo Emerson wrote in his classic essay "Self-Reliance":

> To believe your own thought, to believe that what is true for you in your private heart is true for all men—that is genius. Nothing is at last sacred but the integrity of our own mind . . . Absolve you to yourself, and you shall have the suffrage of the world.

Amen.

And since I'm apparently going full speed ahead on this tangent already, Ralph Waldo Emerson also said, "This time, like all times, is a good one, if we but know what to do with it."

The technology space continues to grow with new apps and social media outlets every day. We, as humans, are growing with it but are struggling to find a way to use it without losing control, becoming compulsive, letting it affect our friendships, our relationships, and most importantly, ourselves. The answer is not to cancel our Instagram accounts, deactivate our Facebook profiles, and delete our Twitter handles. Instead, we must figure out how to use these facts of life as positive forces instead of damaging ones. And we have to figure out how to stay true to the "integrity of our own minds" and not get carried away by the stream of distraction and insecurity.

Writing this book didn't cure me. Far from it; I am still addicted to my phone, social media, reality television, and my DVR. But I have made some changes. I only allow myself to check my social media at work when I run down to grab my lunch or go to the bathroom. I keep my phone in my bag (or pocket) when I have dinners with friends or family. If I have a night at home, I try to spend at least an hour reading or writing before I turn on the television. One foot in front of the other. That's what it's all about.

We'll reach our full potential when we figure out, as Emerson said, "what to do with it." We won't figure it out right away, but . . . baby steps. I have not yet unfriended my ex, but I did make the decision not to follow her on Instagram. I'm getting there.

ACKNOWLEDGMENTS

I am deeply grateful to my editor and friend, Shannon Welch, for her confidence in this project and for standing by it from beginning to end. Without her, it truly would not have come to fruition. Shannon saw the strength in the early manuscript when even I did not and never stopped pushing me to make it everything it could be. Her attention to detail and ability to help me find my voice are things I will always be grateful for. I want to thank Scribner for believing in my manuscript and ultimately me; and also for putting an unparalleled, amazing, thoughtful, and insightful team behind it. Thank you to Nan Graham, who led the amazing team who published *Unfriending My Ex,* and to Roz Lippel, Kara Watson, Brian Belfiglio, Lauren Lavelle, Caitlin Dohrenwend, Elisa Rivlin, Hadley Walker, Tal Goretsky, and John Glynn.

I want to thank my loyal agent and friend Steve Troha for navigating the last four years with me and for introducing me to all of the right people to work with on this project. I am eternally grateful for the constant support and enthusiasm of Lynn Goldberg, Katie Wainwright, Jeff Umbro, Megan Beatie, and Angela Baggetta. Thank you for believing in my book and helping me make it a success.

I want to thank all of the people I spoke to about the topic and the many experts, journalists, and other authors whom I consulted during the process. While there are many names in the footnotes that I am grateful for, special thanks go to Elias Aboujaoude, whose book *Virtually You* was a constant source of information and insight; William Powers, author of *Hamlet's BlackBerry*, who met with me to discuss the topic and his findings; Gary Small, whose columns in *Psychology Today* and other work provided great statistics and information; and Keane Angle, whose interview provided insight from the digital and social marketing perspective. Thank you also to Henry David Thoreau and *Walden,* which got me through my digital detox and continues to change how I see the world around me. I, of course, want to thank every single person who filled out and participated in the hundreds of surveys that gave me a wealth of information about our generation and this topic. I am so grateful that people took the time to answer my sometimes very strange questions.

Thank you to the Brearley School in New York City for giving me the best education I can imagine and for teaching me how to be successful. Brearley gave me the confidence, strength, and hardworking nature to believe that I could succeed at all of my endeavors, even if it meant having two or sometimes three careers at one time. I want to especially thank Mrs. Helaine Smith for her brilliance and for teaching me how to put my voice down onto a page.

Deserving her own start to a paragraph is my dear friend, Dr. Amy Wicker, who, as a doctor of clinical psychology, was a brilliant and incredibly helpful source of knowledge from the human behavioral perspective. On a personal note, I want to thank Amy for being an amazingly loyal friend, who never stopped asking about this project and who has been my sounding board for essentially everything in the past ten years. I am also incredibly grateful for the support of Ken Auletta, Caprice Crane, Jean Vallely Graham, Chris Hardwick, Debbie McEneaney, Roger Rosenblatt, and Alyssa Shelasky who believed in my manuscript and were some of the first people to read it and offer feedback. Thank you to David Silber and everyone at Citigroup for being supportive and understanding of my somewhat double life and to my colleagues for buying this book (you guys did buy the book, right?). I want to thank my friends and colleagues whose lives were constant inspiration and insight, and thank you to *Beverly Hills, 90210* for letting me use the names of their characters to protect the identities of some of my most device-addicted real-life characters. Special thanks to Judgie Graham, Molly Greenberg, Jessica Palmer, Despina Nevells, Keryn Limmer, Sarah Maslin Nir, Peter McEneaney, Emily Calcagnino, Julie Potash Slavin, Randy Slavin, Megan Kelly, Kyle Gilroy, Josephine Bradlee, Nina Braddock, Marina Thompson, Christine Cowan, Chris Sullivan, Erin Reiss Silbert, Lysee Webb, Madison Vain, and the MTV News team. I suppose I should also thank my various exes: without them, this book would be a lot shorter and without a title.

I want to thank my mom and dad who are the best friends and parents I could ask for. Not only did they both provide inspiration and great stories to draw from, but they were supportive every step of the way. Thank you to my dad for giving the best advice, for being my role model, for pushing me to be the best I could be, and for always making me laugh in the best of times and the worst of times. Thank you to my mom for being the warmest and kindest person I've ever met and for her smart and creative mind, which never ceases to amaze me. You are the best and coolest and funniest parents out there. I'm so honored to have you as my best friends.

Last but certainly not least, I want to thank Lexi for being my rock, for always being supportive, and for making every day better. I am ever grateful for the constant laughter, encouragement, and love we share. I should also probably thank you for letting me write a book about my exes. I'm aware that was a bit rude. Thank you for letting me pursue this and all of my dreams and for being one of them. And finally, thank you to Izzy and Emme, the amazing Stolz dogs, for being the best additions to a family anyone could ask for. I forgive you for falling asleep every time I try to read you this book.

NOTES

1: The Experiment

6   "withdrawal." Merriam-Webster.com. Merriam-Web-
    ster, n.d., 15 Jan. 2014. http://www.merriam-webster
    .com/dictionary/withdrawal.

19 *"the simplest programs":* Benny Evangelista, "Attention
    Loss Feared as High-Tech Rewires Brain," *San Francisco
    Chronicle*, November 15, 2009. http://www.sfgate.com
    /cgi-bin/article.cgi?f=/c/a/2009/11/14/BUNI1AB1G2
    .DTL.

2: Generation, Interrupted

41 *"the same neural pathways":* Gary Small, "Techno Ad-
    dicts," PsychologyToday.com, July 22, 2009. http://www
    .psychologytoday.com/blog/brain-bootcamp/200907/
    techno-addicts.

41 *some in the psychiatric community:* Bill Davidow, "Inter-
    net Compulsion Disorder: Should We Include It in the
    DSM?," *Atlantic*, December 13, 2011. http://www.the

atlantic.com/health/archive/2011/12/internet-compulsion-disorder-should-we-include-it-in-the-dsm/249905/.

41   *the tech giant Cisco surveyed members:* Cisco, "Toothpaste, Toilet Paper, and Texting—Say Good Morning to Gen Y," press release, December 12, 2012. http://newsroom.cisco.com/release/1114955.

41–42   *Keane Angle, a digital strategist at 360i:* Keane Angle, e-mail interview with the author, July 26, 2011.

42   *"the constant checking":* Matt Richtel, "It Don't Mean a Thing If You Ain't Got That Ping," *New York Times*, April 22, 2007. http://www.nytimes.com/2007/04/22/weekinreview/22richtel.html?_r=1.

42   *"accustomed to a constant stream":* Ibid.

43   *"The more we become used to":* Evangelista, "Attention Loss Feared."

43   *In his comprehensive and entertaining book:* Elias Aboujaoude, *Virtually You: The Dangerous Powers of the E-Personality* (New York: W. W. Norton, 2011), 210.

43   *Aboujaoude notes a 2004 study:* Ibid., 210–11.

44   *"exhibit signs and symptoms:"* Larry D. Rosen, "Face the Facts: We Are All Headed for an iDisorder," Lifehack.org, March 28, 2012. http://www.lifehack.org/articles/lifehack/face-the-facts-we-are-all-headed-for-an-idisorder.html.

44   *"Drug addicts don't think":* Richtel, "It Don't Mean a Thing."

44 *My friend Dr. Amy Wicker:* The CAGE questionnaire was developed by Dr. John Ewing. CAGE is an internationally used assessment instrument for identifying problems with alcoholism. "The CAGE Questionnaire," *JAMA*, 252, 1905-1907.

46 *"There is something satisfying":* William Powers, interview with the author, November 10, 2011.

47 *The constant distractions and all our time online:* Matt Richtel, "Growing Up Digital, Wired for Distraction," *New York Times*, November 21, 2010. http://www.ny times.com/2010/11/21/technology/21brain.html?.

48 *According to a 2011 study by Cisco:* Stacey Higginbotham, "Social Media, Multi-tasking & Ending Billable Hours," GigaOm.com, September 21, 2011. http://gigaom. com/2011/09/21/social-media-multi-tasking-and-the -death-of-the-billable-hour/. See also: "Cisco Connected World Technology Report," http://www.cisco.com/c/en/ us/solutions/enterprise/connected-world-technology -report/index.html#~2012.

48 *Further, a recent study of university students:* Eyal Ophir et al., "Cognitive Control in Media Multitaskers," *Proceedings of the National Academy of Sciences of the United States of America*, August 24, 2009. http:// www.pnas.org/content/early/2009/08/21/0903620106 .abstract.

49 *"processing multiple incoming streams":* Ibid.

49 *"mythical activity in which people believe":* Edward M. Hallowell, *Crazy Busy: Overstretched, Overbooked, and*

About to Snap! Strategies for Handling Your Fast-Paced Life (New York: Ballantine Books, 2007).

49 *why some companies are now preventing:* Emily Glazer, "P&G Curbs Employees' Internet Use," *Wall Street Journal*, April 4, 2012. http://online.wsj.com/article/SB1000 142405270230407200457732414284700634O.html.

49 *"The same inefficiency that freezes":* Richard E. Cytowic, "The Key to Efficient Multitasking: One Thing at a Time," *Fallible Mind* (blog), *Psychology Today*, March 23, 2013. http://www.psychologytoday.com/blog/the-fallible-mind/201203/the-key-efficient-multitasking-one-thing-time.

49 *scientists in California found:* Matt Richtel, "Digital Devices Deprive Brain of Needed Downtime," *New York Times*, August 24, 2010. http://www.nytimes.com/2010/08/25/technology/25brain.html.

50 *"memory can be boosted":* Sarah O'Meara, "'Wakeful Resting' More Effective Than Crosswords to Fight Memory Loss," *Huffington Post UK*, July 24, 2012. http://www.huffingtonpost.co.uk/2012/07/24/wakeful-resting-more-effective-crosswords_n_1697311.html?ir=UK+Lifestyle.

50 *A University of Michigan study revealed:* Richtel, "Digital Devices Deprive Brain."

3: Facebook Is Ruining My Life

60 *In an article titled:* Leon Neyfakh, "The Power of Lonely," *The Boston Globe,* March 6, 2012. Retrieved from

http://www.boston.com/bostonglobe/ideas/articles/
2011/03/06/the_power_of_lonely/?page=1.

61 *Nielsen found that between 2003 and 2009:* Nielsen-
Wire, "Report: Social Media and Video Site Engagement Reshapes the Web," April 22, 2009. http://blog
.nielsen.com/nielsenwire/nielsen-news/online
-global-landscape-0409/.

61 *"growing at a rate":* NielsenWire, "New Mobile Obsession: U.S. Teens Triple Data Usage," December 15,
2011.   http://blog.nielsen.com/nielsenwire/online_
mobile/new-mobile-obsession-u-s-teens-triple-data-
usage/.

61 *They also found that the average teenager:* Ibid.

61 *25 percent of teens:* Common Sense Media, "Is Technology Networking Changing Childhood?" press release,
August 10, 2009. http://www.commonsensemedia.org
/about-us/news/press-releases/social-networking-
changing-childhood.

62 *Americans in general spent:* Nielsen, *State of the Media:
The Social Media Report, Q3 2011,* September 9, 2011.
http://cn.nielsen.com/documents/Nielsen-Social-
Media-Report_FINAL_090911.pdf.

63 *A June 2011 Pew Research Center poll:* Pew Internet
and American Life Project, "Americans and Their Cell
Phones," August 15, 2011. http://www.pewinternet
.org/Press-Releases/2011/Cell-Phones-2011.aspx.

63 *31 percent of American adults:* Pew Internet and American Life Project, "Americans and Text Messaging," Sep-

tember 19, 2011. http://pewinternet.org/Reports/2011/Cell-Phone-Texting-2011.aspx.

64 *"emotional closeness declines":* Robin Dunbar, "You've Got to Have (150) Friends," *New York Times*, December 25, 2010. http://www.nytimes.com/2010/12/26/opinion/26dunbar.html.

66 *For instance, compared to students:* http://ns.umich.edu/new/releases/7724.

69 *a number of people described:* Jenna Wortham, "The Facebook Resisters," *New York Times,* December 13, 2011. http://www.nytimes.com/2011/12/14/technology/shunning-facebook-and-living-to-tell-about-it.html.

71 *"the faux friendships of Facebook":* Bill Keller, "Wising Up to Facebook," *New York Times*, June 10, 2012. http://www.nytimes.com/2012/06/11/opinion/wising-up-to-facebook.html?_r=0.

72 *believes that our generation is lonelier:* Tom Meltzer, "Social Networking: Failure to Connect," *Guardian*, August 6, 2010. http://www.guardian.co.uk/media/2010/aug/07/social-networking-friends-lonely.

72 *In an aptly titled* Atlantic *article:* Stephen Marche, "Is Facebook Making Us Lonely?" *Atlantic*, May 1, 2012.

72 *In 2010, the UK-based:* Mental Health Foundation, "The Lonely Society?" May 2010.

72 *In a medical study printed in* Pediatrics: Gwen Schurgin O'Keefe, Kathleen Clarke-Pearson, and Council on Communications and Media, "The Impact of Social Media

on Children, Adolescents, and Families," *Pediatrics* 127 (2011): 800. http://pediatrics.aappublications.org /content/early/2011/03/28/peds.2011-0054.abstract.

73   *"[Facebook is] creating a den":* Daniel Gulati, "Facebook Is Making Us Miserable," *Harvard Business Review*, HBR Blog Network, December 9, 2011.

4: We're "Friends"

84   *examined how honest we are:* Meltzer, "Social Networking."

87   *"With so much of our facts readily available":* Aboujaoude, *Virtually You*, 238.

88   *One study completed at Western Illinois University:* Chenda Ngak, "Number of Facebook Friends Linked to Narcissism, Says Study," CBSNews.com, March 20, 2012. http://www.cbsnews.com/news/facebook-may-cause -stress-study-says/.

88   *humans cannot process more than:* Aleks Krotoski, "Robin Dunbar: We Can Only Ever Have 150 Friends at Most . . . ," *Guardian Observer*, March 13, 2010. http://www.guardian.co.uk/technology/2010/mar/14 /my-bright-idea-robin-dunbar.

99   *"You may find a time":* Emily Post Institute, "Online Friending Etiquette," Accessed 2012. http://www.emily post.com/social-life/social-networking/140-online -friending-etiquette-myspace-facebook.

5:

111 *"desensitization makes us bypass"*: Aboujadoude, *Virtually You*, 107 (quoting Dr. Jeanne B. Funk).

111 *"we escape the consequences"*: Dr. Amy Wicker, interview with the author, November 13, 2011.

111 *"empathy deficit may not be limited"*: Gary Small and Gigi Vorgan, "Is the Internet Killing Empathy?," CNN.com, February 18, 2011. http://www.cnn.com/2011/OPINION/02/18/small.vorgan.internet.empathy/index.html?hpt=C2.

112 *"Gentleness, common courtesy, and the little niceties"*: Aboujaoude, *Virtually You*, 96.

112 *"our online self is also dangerous"*: Ibid., 20.

116 *"When people tease or bully"*: Robin M. Kowalski, "Cyber Bullying: Recognizing and Treating Victim and Aggressor," *Psychiatric Times*, October 1, 2008. http://www.psychiatrictimes.com/print/article/10168/1336550.

122 *A designer by the name of Lee Byron:* http://www.leebyron.com/what/breakups/.

122 *Further, a 2011 study by a market research firm:* Chris Matyszczyk, "One-Third Have Broken Up by Facebook, Text or E-mail—Survey," CNET.com, November 13, 2011, http://news.cnet.com/8301-17852_3-57323837-71/one-third-have-broken-up-by-facebook-text-or-e-mail-survey/; Lab42, "The Relationships Status Update," Lab42 blog, November 4, 2011, http://blog.lab42.com/the-relationship-status-update.

7: Unfriending My Ex

141   *"People consider their online sexual relationships":*
Aaron Ben-Zeév, PhD, "Is Chatting Cheating?," *Psychology Today,* September 5, 2008. http://www.psycholog
ytoday.com/blog/in-the-name-love/200809/is-chatting
-cheating.

148   *Some lawyers are calling Facebook:* John Stevens, "The
Facebook Divorces: Social Network Site Is Cited in "a
THIRD of Splits,'" *Daily Mail,* December 30, 2011.
http://www.dailymail.co.uk/femail/article-2080398
/Facebook-cited-THIRD-divorces.html.

148   *the American Academy of Matrimonial Lawyers announced:* Carl Bialik, "Irreconcilable Claim: Facebook
Causes 1 in 5 Divorces," *Wall Street Journal,* March 12,
2011. http://online.wsj.com/article/SB10001424052748
703597804576194563288753204.html.

148   *The same study found that Facebook:* David Gardner,
"The Marriage Killer: One in Five American Divorces
Now Involve Facebook," *Daily Mail,* December 1, 2010.
http://www.dailymail.co.uk/news/article-1334482
/The-marriage-killer-One-American-divorces-involve
-Facebook.html.

149   *In her online column:* Pamela Haag, "Is Facebook the
Petri Dish of Jealousy in Your Love Life?," *Marriage 3.0*
(blog), *Psychology Today,* April 12, 2012. http://www
.psychologytoday.com/blog/marriage-30/201204/is
-facebook-the-petri-dish-jealousy-in-your-love-life.

152 *An MTV initiative called A Thin Line:* http://www. norc.org/NewsEventsPublications/PressReleases/Pages/ mtv-associated-press-norc-center-survey-finds-that-on line-bullying-has-declined-young-people-are-making -better-digital.aspx.

153 *Google mobile application called Latitude:* www.google .com/latitude.

154 *In August 2009, an off-duty cop:* Edward Marshall, "City Officer Charged," *Journal* (Martinsburg, WV), August 11, 2009. http://www.journal-news.net/page/content .detail/id/523593.html.

154 *His story is benign compared to that:* Staff, "Father Stabbed Estranged Wife to Death After She Changed Her Facebook Status to 'Single,'" *Daily Mail*, January 23, 2009. http://www.dailymail.co.uk/news/article -1126872/Father-stabbed-estranged-wife-death -changed-Facebook-status-single.html.

155 *Just last year, a Philadelphia man:* http://www.web pronews.com/man-stabs-wife-in-the-face-over-a-face book-like-2013-04.

155 *Another woman ended up dead:* Staff, "Jealous Husband Murdered Wife and Killed Himself with Electric Drill After She Ended Marriage on Facebook," *Daily Mail*, February 11, 2009, http://www.dailymail.co.uk /news/article-1141594/Jealous-husband-murdered -wife-killed-electric-drill-ended-marriage-Facebook .html.

155   *And finally, a long-distance relationship:* Milton Bra-
      fado, "3 Sad Cases of Facebook Spousal Jealousy That
      Lead [sic] to Murder," *Yahoo! Voices*, March 31, 2010.
      http://voices.yahoo.com/3-sad-cases-facebook-spousal
      -jealousy-5748394.html.

161   *"DSM-certified narcissists":* Aboujaoude, *Virtually You*, 68.

162   *Dr. Aboujaoude argues that the number:* Ibid., 69.

169   *"an exaggerated sense of our abilities":* Ibid., 11.

9: Baby Steps

182   *"Reality television programs":* Valerie Strauss, "SAT
      Question on Reality TV Stirs Controversy," *Answer Sheet*
      (blog), *Washington Post*, March 15, 2011. http://www
      .washingtonpost.com/blogs/answer-sheet/post/sat
      -question-on-reality-tv-stirs-controversy/2011/03/15
      /ABjNyCY_blog.html.

183   *"We don't have a choice":* Erik Qualman, "Social
      Media Revolution," YouTube video, June 8, 2011.
      http://www.youtube.com/watch?feature=player
      _embedded&v=3SuNx0UrnEo.

189   *"I spend way too much time":* Edna Gundersen, "Will
      the Rolling Stones Launch a Tour in 2012?," *USA
      Today*, September 19, 2011. http://usatoday30.usa
      today.com/life/music/news/story/2011-09-19/rolling
      -stones/50467346/1.

189   *"Look at the bad decisions"*: Huffington Post, "Arianna Huffington, Nicholas Carr Discuss the Need to 'Unplug and Recharge' on *Morning Joe*," HuffingtonPost.com video, June 14, 2010. http://www.huffingtonpost.com/2010/06/14/internet-addiction-nichol_n_611321.html.